WHEN THE WORLD ENDED

EMMA LECONTE

WHEN

THE WORLD ENDED

The Diary of

EMMA LeCONTE

Edited by Earl Schenck Miers

Foreword by Anne Firor Scott

University of Nebraska Press
Lincoln and London

First Bison Book Printing: 1987

Library of Congress Cataloging-in-Publication Data
LeConte, Emma.
  When the world ended
  Reprint. Originally published: New York: Oxford
University Press, 1957.
  Includes Index.
    1. LeConte, Emma—Diaries. 2. South Carolina—
History—Civil War, 1861–1865—Personal Narratives.
3. Columbia (S.C.)—History. 4. United States—History—
Civil War, 1861–1865—Personal narratives, Confederate.
5. Sherman's March through the Carolinas—Personal
narratives. 6. Columbia (S.C.)—Biography. I. Miers,
Earl Schenck, 1910–1972. II. Title.
E605.L46A3   1987   973.7′82   87-5937
ISBN 0-8032-8151-X (pbk.)

For

Barbara and Larry Linck

with affection

FOREWORD
By Anne Firor Scott

When Emma Leconte's wartime diary was first published in 1957 it was hailed as a rare picture of the experiences and emotions of southerners living in Sherman's path as he headed north after his triumphant march through Georgia. It allows us to witness firsthand the fearful anticipations of the citizens of Columbia, who well know that Sherman has no love for South Carolinians but who cannot be sure just where he and his army are headed. When the Union army finally arrives, we see the range of reactions that always characterize people in a crisis and witness the astonishing resilience of human beings under stress. Its value as such a document is undiminished.

But the diary offers much more than a new insight into the civilian side of the war's last bitter days in the South. It is an impressive literary creation that reveals some of the characteristic social structures and attitudes of the southern upper class at midcentury. It tells us, as well, a good deal about certain kinds of southern women.

Thinking back in her old age, Emma LeConte could not remember exactly how she began to write.

I suppose it was a kind of New Year's start that would have been dropped but that events crowded with so much of horror and disaster that I could but try to chronicle them. It was written on pieces of brownish Confederate letter paper. I took it with me when I married and finding it was wearing to pieces, and much of it being in pencil, was fading into illegibility, I undertook to copy it, or at least most of it, what seemed of any general interest.[1]

Written at moments of high emotion (excitement, fear, fury, hope, and hopelessness), Emma LeConte's prose is nonetheless controlled and ordered, and her vocabulary bears witness to much reading. Toward the end we are not surprised to find her turning to Gibbon and Michelet to escape the despair of post-Sherman Columbia. Her evocative description of the coming of spring to the South Carolina countryside in April 1865 will stir memories in any southerner (p. 86). The family walk in the moonlight through ruined Columbia brings home the reality of invasion and destruction as no abstract description is likely to do (pp. 99–100).

She handles the inner world with equal skill, noticing her own changes of feeling and reactions to the things happening around her. "How one grows accustomed to things—a year ago all this would have made me half crazy with anxiety . . . now it all seems natural," she notes as the city waits for Sherman to show his hand (p. 26). Then, as it is clear that he is approaching: "I do not feel half so frightened as I thought I would" (p. 30). Much later she records a feeling of dull apathy and interprets it as the natural reaction to a long period of high excitement. We feel with her the hopelessness of the days following Lincoln's assassination (at which the family had rejoiced) when no one knows what will come next.

Less consciously, she illuminates the prevailing attitudes toward the black people. At the beginning of 1865 slavery is still in place and the LeContes take for granted the services of their house slaves as well as the loyalty of the more than sixty on the plantation in Liberty County. Emma perceives Henry, one of the house slaves, as faithful and indispensable, and reports that in the immediate aftermath of the fire it is the slaves who keep the family from starving. Yet her offhand comments reveal deep-seated racism. She sees the blacks as unchangeably inferior, and when they begin to leave, the fact that they have saved the family from the worst consequences of Sherman's destruction does not prevent her from heaping scorn upon them. "I wish she [her mother] would get clear of all of them— we have to feed them and get very little out of them in return." The idea of a Negro regiment coming to occupy the town horrifies her; the Fourth of July celebration of the freed people she characterizes as a "horrid degradation," calling the blacks a "motley throng" (p. 114). Their songs, which she must have heard all her life, now are "strange" and their dances "weird" (p. 115).

She describes with appropriate irony the Ladies' Bazaar, incongruously conducted as the town hunkers down to prepare for Sherman. She does not mention—and perhaps does not understand—the enormous contribution Soldiers' Aid societies had made during the preceding four years by just such efforts. Confederate women working together in these societies had bought gunboats, outfitted regiments, and provisioned hospitals. People, then as now, preferred to feel they were getting something for their contributions to a good cause, no matter how ridiculous the "something" was, and the women had learned to take advantage of this fact.

We see kinship—one of the vital social structures of the southern aristocracy—running like a continuous thread through this diary. The family was embedded in a kin network that stretched from Philadelphia to middle and southeast Georgia, and included grandparents, uncles, aunts and cousins to the third degree. These relatives form the chief part of LeConte social life.

There is ample evidence here of the fierce patriotism of many southerners in the early days of the war, some of which survived to the very end. Hope died hard, and even after Lincoln's assassination we find Emma fantasizing about rescue from England or France.

Through it all the young diarist is aware of creating a record for the future. She conscientiously describes her coarse underclothing "such as we gave to the negroes formerly," the meager food upon which the family subsisted, the pleasure of finding one skein of good wool from which to knit stockings, or happiness that lies in a new pair of shoes.

Keepers of journals, whether they mean to or not, always paint their own portraits, and this one is no exception. We see Emma LeConte clearly enough to want to know much more. Who was this young woman who could write with such vigor and force at the age of seventeen? And what happened to her after the diary ends? Fortunately, thanks in part to her own efforts, a record exists that permits us to answer some of these questions.[2]

Emma LeConte was the daughter of Joseph LeConte and Caroline Elizabeth Nisbet LeConte, known as Bessie, both natives of southeast Georgia. The LeConte brothers, John and Joseph, were among the handful of distinguished southern scientists living and working in the South when the Civil War began. Raised by an unusually erudite planter father, they had studied at the University of Georgia in Athens, and after intermediate careers elsewhere had joined the faculty of that institution. Conflicts between the university president and many members of the faculty led the brothers to move to South Carolina College in Columbia, where Emma spent her childhood and where her younger sisters were born.

The LeContes were well-established members of the planter aristocracy, and the family was easily accepted in Columbia, where a little circle of southern intelligentsia was often enlivened by the meetings of the South Carolina legislature with its colorful fire-eaters and occasional planter-statesmen. Years later, though he was well acquainted with Cambridge, Philadelphia, and Berkeley, Joseph LeConte would say he had never found such congenial society as that of Columbia in the 1850s. LeConte himself was a man of broad interests that included poetry, literature, and art, as well as science. Like his daughter, he wrote journals and autobiographical volumes of sparkling prose.[3] In this stimulating atmosphere Emma spent twelve years.

While formal education, especially higher education, for women was rare in the 1850s, Emma LeConte was not unique in her unusual degree of learning. The phenomenon of a scholar father raising his daughter to emulate his own accomplishments went back at least to the eighteenth century, and examples could be found north and south in the years when Emma was growing up.[4]

As the eldest child in a family where there was yet no son, she early became her father's intellectual companion. Her precocity delighted him. There was a family story, for example, about the time he took her walking on a beach in Massachusetts. Hotel guests were astonished when Emma returned reciting the scientific names of all the shells she had gathered. She was then three and a half.

Bessie LeConte was a worrier who was often discontented and had some difficulty in expressing warmth and affection. The fact that Joseph and his daughter were both demonstrative and given to good cheer drew them together. From an early age he, rather than her self-effacing mother, was Emma's model.

The curriculum that Joseph LeConte designed for his daughter included Latin, Greek, French, and German, as well as mathematics and modern languages. Intermittently, she went to school—but except for an occasional unusual teacher she found such formal education as her environment offered deficient, especially when compared with the instruction she had at home. The combination of what she learned in various schools, her father's tutoring, and her capacity for systematic independent study had made her the model of an educated woman at an early age. More than sixty years later she would recall an occasion when a young man, escorting her to a dance, spoke learnedly about philosophy, science, and other abstruse subjects. A year or two afterward, when they had become good friends, she asked him why he had undertaken such serious conversation in such circumstances, to which he replied that he had heard so many accounts of her learning and intellectuality that he had been afraid to broach lighter topics.

The diary ends in August 1865—but already we can sense the amazing resilience of human beings in adversity as we see Emma returning to her French and German and conic sections, and noting that the family is already getting used to living under military occupation. While her father was desperately trying to find ways to support his family, the college reopened, reorganized as a university. He was once again employed, and young men who had survived the war came back to take up their interrupted education.

Emma, meantime, was going through a recognizable stage of adolescence. As is often the case with highly intellectual girls, she saw herself as a wallflower who would probably never have a beau. Then, *mirable dictu*, a young man announced himself to be in love with her.

The power to inspire admiration gave a sense of ease and confidence which the teasing of my younger cousin Johnny could not destroy. . . . The effect was quite magical. My awkwardness and mauvaise honte dropped from me like a cloak and from that time on I gave myself unreservedly to the intoxication of social dissipation . . . there was no further lack of success.[5]

The "social dissipation" consisted principally of dances where—due to the hard times—no refreshments were served, but each young man gave fifty cents to the black fiddlers who provided the music.

Among those who took part in these dances was a returning veteran who was taking courses with her father, a young man well known to the family since he had grown up close to the Nisbets' home in Georgia. In later years Emma suggested that she had not been particularly enthusiastic about marrying Farish Furman, but that her mother and aunts, seeing him as an appropriate match for her, had pressed his suit with such enthusiasm that, almost without intending to, she had allowed herself to become engaged.

Meantime, Joseph LeConte at forty-two, all his papers destroyed, faced the seemingly hopeless task of rebuilding a scientific career from the ground up. The University of South Carolina was caught up in the postwar debate over the proper education of black people. Along with the rest of the white faculty, Joseph LeConte did not approve of admitting freedmen to the university, but however that question might be resolved, resources were apt to be scarce for the foreseeable future. Scientists in the North—among them Louis Agassiz, who had once said Joseph LeConte was his best student—tried to help, but prejudices against a man who had served the Confederacy were strong. Finally, invitations to both the LeConte brothers to join the faculty of the new University of California offered a way out, and just as Emma's engagement became formal the rest of the family prepared to move west, leaving her to marry and move farther south.

The young people went to live on a large plantation in middle Georgia, which Farish Furman had inherited from his grandfather. The available society was a far cry from the lively prewar life in Columbia, and isolation and loneliness bore heavily upon Emma, as did the birth of stillborn twins. The real problem, however, was the intensity of the tie between this young woman and her father. She thought him the most perfect man she had ever known, and late in life would still write: "My dear father was always the centre of my life—in him love, reverence, even adoration united. In a wonderful way he excited all this and at the same time, such companionship! such educational influence!"[6] She felt their separation deeply and urged her husband to move west. Farish Furman was not inclined to leave his legal and political career in Georgia. He was also caught up in experiments in scientific agriculture that would bring him a good deal of acclaim in the agricultural and "New South" press. Doubtless he was in no hurry, either, to move closer to the father whom his wife admired so extravagantly that he himself was likely to feel inadequate by comparison.[7]

Emma had to content herself with taking her daughters (born in 1872 and 1874) for long visits in Berkeley. On one of these she kept a journal of a trip with her father and cousin and a few others into the High Sierra. Her literary and descriptive powers had continued to develop, along with a gentle wit.

In 1883, when Emma was thirty-seven, Farish Furman contracted malaria and died. His wife took over the plantation and the education of her daughters, and conducted both with considerable success.

She added another contribution to her self-portrait when she was seventy-one and living with her daughter, Bess, in Macon, Georgia. At Christmas 1917 her son-in-law—perhaps with some intention of encouraging her to record her observations of another war—had given her a large diary. Though expressing doubt on the first page that "an old woman" could have anything of interest to say, in fact she was soon writing away, creating another interesting manuscript.[8] The First World War, of course, did not come home as had the Civil War, so while she writes feelingly about fuel shortages, as the temperature drops below freezing and her daughter scrapes coal dust from the floor of the coal house, the physical suffering was nothing compared to that of 1865. She pays close attention to European politics and the progress of the war, but for the most part she is preoccupied with religious observance, Red Cross work, and with her extended family.

In 1918 as in 1865 she knits socks for soldiers, worries about threats of epidemics, and is a fervent patriot, though this time her patriotism is that of an American, not a southerner. She is deeply involved in the work of the women's societies of two churches, and teaches Bible study intermittently. Her diary is filled with outlines for these classes, which demonstrate a profound familiarity with the Scriptures. With her daughter, she works hard and regularly for the Red Cross, and goes, also, to suffrage meetings. When the Suffrage Amendment passes the House of Representatives in March 1918, she calls the fact "grand news" and says Bess is jubilant. "Not an 'anti' peeped!" she chortles after she and Bess have done a little suffrage proselyting at a Red Cross meeting. "We discovered, however, while taking off our uniforms that Mrs. Foster is secretly much interested in the Cause, though she dared not speak out . . . Bess expects to make a convert of her" (Feb. 1, 1918).

Among her church-related activities is a school for black

children. She urges her affluent friends to help the "little Negro children working without desks and blackboards and with insufficient fires" (Jan. 28, 1918). She calls this work her "mission" and prays for strength to keep it up.

Another indication of her changed perception of black people appears in the spring: "All day at the Auxiliary meeting . . . the whole meeting was a great improvement on all previous ones in spirituality and earnestness . . . A Negro priest talked to us of his work—a great advance on the 1912 meeting when the women in Macon refused to have Archdeacon Henderson talk to them" (April 17, 1918).

As she had unconsciously depicted a way of life in 1865, so she does in 1918. With both daughters and many relatives living close by, she is embedded in a kin network that provides a comfortable setting in which to grow old. She reads to her grandchildren as her father had read to her, and watches their development with the greatest interest.

Money is scarce, but she is able to contribute to causes she believes in and, with some sacrifice, to make gifts to needy relatives. Both daughters have married professional men who are able to afford automobiles before the day of Henry Ford, and are sufficiently influential to be able to procure scarce coal to keep the family warm. As she records her daily activity, it is easy to see the increased mobility the automobile made possible.

Perhaps the most important insight the 1918 diary provides is how little the war affected daily life unless some family member was actually in the army. We can see, too, how important visiting still was in the lives of middle-class women. Although Bess Furman Talley was extremely busy with church and Red Cross and suffrage work, she and her mother rarely pass a day without a visit to some friend or relative. Black domestic servants in the kitchen make volunteer work and all the visits possible.

By a curious coincidence, this wartime diary ends, as had the earlier one, in August. The final pages contain detailed notes for several Bible study classes.

Emma LeConte Furman was in her mid-seventies when she was persuaded to write a final contribution to the history of her time, recollections of her childhood and early adulthood. Again, it was her son-in-law, Nicholas Talley, who pressed her to write. She resisted at first, saying that her mind, unlike most old people's, did not dwell on the past

> perhaps because there is so much I want to forget. In looking back there has always been the danger of self-pity and so I never encouraged looking back. Not that one regrets past suffering. I have learned to be most thankful for the suffering—but that is what one remembers most vividly and that is just what one can not share with anyone.[9]

However, once she began the words seemed to flow easily and for the third time she created an important record of a world that, by the time she wrote, had almost disappeared. Drawing on her memories and family letters, she reconstructed the early lives and the marriage of her parents, her own childhood, and the family setting in which she had grown up. She drew incisive portraits of individuals. For example, John LeConte's wife, Josephine, was one of the most beautiful women she had even known. Emma had been both attracted by her beauty and repelled by her egotism. Josephine emerges from Emma's pages in full glory as she gathers her admirers in the legislature around the tea table in Columbia and persuades them to build just the house she most desires on the college campus. The memoirs make it clear that Emma's relationship with her mother had been a troubled one, and emphasize over and over her close attachment to her father.

Looking back, she uses the term "Civil War" (at a time when southern children were still being sternly enjoined that it had been "The War between the States") and notes that after reflection and reading Woodrow Wilson's *History of the American People* she had concluded that there had been "fanaticism on both sides." She adds that "with coolness and freedom from prejudice and passion" the war might have been avoided, especially if southerners had realized that the world had outgrown slavery. She reflects upon her own fanaticism, and says that there were few cool heads at the time.

In her old age Emma had become enough of a feminist not only to cheer the passage of the suffrage amendment but to remember with dismay her mother's disappointment at the birth of a third and then a fourth girl—when she had hoped for a son. She also writes scornfully of the unwillingness of southern families to "teach women anything which might be a source of independence." Unfortunately, the document ends just as she marries Farish Furman, leaving to the energy of some future historian the reconstruction of her life as a postwar planter.

Born in 1847, Emma LeConte Furman lived until 1932. Through all those years of wars, reconstruction, and depression, she had gone through the standard roles: daughter, wife, mother, and some not so standard ones: planter and gifted writer. She was a highly intelligent, well-educated woman—and in the end religion came to mean more to her than anything else. (Despite her Presbyterian beginnings, she had become an ardent Episcopalian.) We are not likely to know the cause of the suffering of which she spoke so feelingly in the first pages of her reminiscence, nor to understand fully how the young girl of the 1865 diary, hoping that the pleasures of life had not altogether passed her by, became the old woman so preoccupied with the state of her soul that she could speak of herself—in her seventies—as still struggling to overcome sin. She, like the society of which she was a part, changed over time in fascinating ways, and died hoping to reestablish her close relationship with her father when she got to heaven.

NOTES

1. "Recollections of Emma Florence LeConte's Youth," copy of typescript in the possession of Professor Lester D. Stephens of the University of Georgia.

2. The material in this introduction rests heavily upon manuscript material collected by Professor Stephens when he was preparing his definitive biography of Joseph LeConte. I am immensely grateful to Professor Stephens for lending this material and for reading this essay in manuscript. A vast quantity of family letters scattered in several depositories could provide the data for a biography of Emma LeConte.

3. During the time Joseph LeConte was making his way to south Georgia to rescue his daughter Sallie and his sister from Sherman's troops he somehow managed to keep a journal of his adventures. Published under the odd title *'Ware Sherman* (Berkeley, 1937) it is an extraordinary piece of reporting. His *Autobiography* (New York, 1903) was published after his death.

4. For example, Jane Colden, daughter of Cadwallader Colden, who became a gifted botanist under her father's tutelage, and Theodosia Burr, whom her father, Aaron Burr, set out to make the most learned woman in America. See also Walter Rundell, Jr., ed. "'If Fortune Should Fail': Civil War Letters of Dr. Samuel D. Sanders," *South Carolina Historical Magazine*, 65 (July and October 1964): 131–33, 140–44, 218–29. Langdon Cheves, a fellow South Carolinian, like Joseph LeConte had concentrated a good deal on the education

of his daughter Louisa, who became one of the leading women in the state. Many of the nineteenth-century achievers whose biographies appear in *Notable American Women* (Cambridge, 1971) were educated by their fathers.

5. "Recollections," pp. 20–21.

6. Ibid., p. 313.

7. The extraordinary attachment went both ways. Joseph LeConte would write of Emma: "one of the strongest and yet the gentlest, most refined and most beautiful characters I ever knew. It may seem strange, but it is nevertheless true that I not only love but actually reverence my own child." Manuscript autobiography, Southern Historical Collection, University of North Carolina, Chapel Hill, N.C. This comment was omitted from the printed volume. Cited in Lester D. Stephens, *Joseph LeConte* (Baton Rouge, 1982) pp. 109–10. Emma must surely have read this after her father's death, yet in her own reminiscence she would write "Oh if I could only have appreciated his character—the depths of his strong religious nature—and been more influenced by it!—Could have grown what he wished me to be. Are not such prayers surely answered? even if they seem not to be in this life, at least in that to come?"

8. Photocopy of "Diary of Emma LeConte Furman 1918" in possession of Professor Lester D. Stephens.

9. "Reminiscences of Emma LeConte Furman," photocopy of manuscript. The typescript cited above does not include these introductory comments, but is otherwise identical except for the title. It was made by one of her daughters.

CONTENTS

═══════

INTRODUCTION

AFTER more than ninety years, Sherman's march from Atlanta to Savannah, then northward through the Carolinas, remains an episode without parallel in American history. An old precept of war, true in the cases of Sherman (Union) and Morgan (Confederate), prescribes fame for the general who leads an army to bloody victory on the battlefield and infamy for the general who burns a house. But another factor was involved in Sherman's march. After four weary years of war the dream of the South was being smashed. With each fleeting day the areas of possible resistance were vanishing. Yet, always, there was one place where the fight could be carried on as long as breath remained. Within each rebellious heart that had believed so intensely in the cause of the South, that had suffered so valiantly for this cause and had learned so well to hate all who opposed it, surrender continued unthinkable.

Even for the professional historian the opportunities are few to share intimately this kind of emotion, which often motivates the irresistible course of history. To publish for the first time the diary kept by Emma Florence LeConte during these last months of the Confederacy is exciting, for it provides this rare experience. Emma was seventeen years of age when these passionate pages were written, and the war had brought her, she said, 'little of the exuberant joy that people talk about as the natural heritage of youth.' Four years of bitter blood-letting she reduced to a single stark sentence: 'No pleasure, no enjoyment—nothing but rigid economy and hard work—nothing but the stern realities of life.'

Emma was thirteen, living quietly on the drowsy campus of South Carolina College, where her father, Joseph LeConte, taught chemistry, when South Carolina seceded from the Union. Never would she forget that bright April day in 1861 when the church bells of Columbia began to toll in unison. Sumter had been fired on—the South had struck its first blow for independence—and, Emma remembered, 'the whole town was in a joyful tumult.' Soon the boys from the college left in a body to fight for the South, and Emma's father was called to important service as a consulting chemist to the Confederate States Nitre and Mining Bureau. So did the dream begin—for Emma, the beautiful dream, sparkling with youthful romanticism, with sublime faith, with purity of purpose . . .

And now, almost four years later, the crushing end! Who can doubt that as Emma wept into her diary all of the heartbreak and disillusionment which these humiliating hours produced that hers, like Lee's, were 'tears of blood'? With a power of expression far beyond the normal youth, she caught the agonizing immediacy of those months—the fear, the courage, the sense of betrayal, the nothingness of a world torn asunder. Sherman marching into South Carolina . . . with those five cruel words began the realization that the cause was lost, the dream ending, a way of life dying.

Well could Emma believe the wild rumors she heard of how Sherman's performance in Georgia had been only a prelude to the drastic fate he intended for South Carolina. There is abundant evidence that Sherman's army marched northward from Savannah in a vengeful spirit, remembering that South Carolina had been the first state to leave the Union, holding her responsible at Sumter for firing the shot that had brought on this undeclared war between North and South, and wanting above all to teach a lesson to this 'hellhole of secession.' Sherman himself had been quoted as saying he would bring 'every Southern woman to the washtub,' and it is entirely possible that Sherman made that remark, for he had a way of blurting out anything that crossed his lively mind.

Writing home, Chaplain John J. Hight of the 58th Indiana supplied a clue to the temper of Union soldiers as they left Georgia: 'Poor South Carolina must suffer now. Her deluded people will . . . reap the full reward of all their folly and crimes.' Alabama-born Major Henry Hitchcock, serving on Sherman's staff, lacked even this note of compassion, declaring that 'of all the mean humbugs, South Carolina is the meanest.' Yankee scuttle-butters made no secret of the fact that Kilpatrick's cavalry rode out of Savannah with saddlebags bulging with matches.

From day to day, as Sherman's troops approach Columbia, Emma's diary catches the growing, numbing terror of a city that knows not what to expect, and surely never anticipated the havoc that was wrought upon it! For more than ninety years a controversy has existed over who was responsible for the burning of Columbia. Sherman contended that he never gave the order for its fiery destruction, but no South Carolinian who, like Emma, lived through the terrible night of the fire ever believed his story, and one can wonder what solace Sherman expected to provide by suggesting that the tragedy had resulted from nothing more malicious than an act of sheer animal spirit! After the war Sherman was called to testify in some cotton cases (J. J. Browne *v.* The United States), and said:

> *Q:* Were you at any time before crossing the Savannah River, or before reaching Columbia, aware of a spirit of vengeance—a desire of vengeance—animating your troops to be wreaked upon South Carolina?
>
> A: (*Sherman*): I was; the feeling was universal; and pervaded all ranks.
>
> *Q:* Officers and all?
>
> *A:* Officers and all; we looked upon South Carolina as the cause of our woes.
>
> *Q:* And thought she thoroughly deserved strong treatment?
>
> *A:* Yes, sir; that she thoroughly deserved extirpation.

To South Carolinians, reading this evidence, whether or not Sherman gave an actual order to burn Columbia became an academic matter; there were many eyewitnesses, like William Gilmore Simms, to testify that Sherman's 'hellhounds' were

> ... well prepared with all the appliances essential to their work. They did not need the torch. They carried with them,

from house to house, pots and vessels containing combustible liquids, composed probably of phosphorous and other similar agents, turpentine, etc., and with balls of cotton saturated in this liquid, with which they also overspread the floors and walls; they conveyed the flames with wonderful rapidity from dwelling to dwelling. Each had his ready box of Lucifer matches, and, with a scrape upon the walls, the flames began to rage. Where houses were closely contiguous, a brand from one was the means of conveying destruction to the other. . . .

When at last Sherman and his soldiers marched on, there was touching poignancy in Emma's description of the devastated city. It was small wonder that the stricken girl saw Sherman as a robber and an incendiary, and yet, for the dispassionate historian, it is difficult to find among the generals of the North one who became more intrinsically the friend of the South than William Tecumseh Sherman. Unhappily, the South found reason to hate him twice, though between these two poles of unpopularity there were a number of years when many Southerners almost forgave his pyrotechnical peregrinations. Contradictions similar to this, however, became as natural to Billy Sherman as his flaming red hair and fierce, shaggy beard.

Four years of Sherman's youth were spent at Fort Moultrie on Sullivan's Island, within easy reach of Charleston. Letters home described how fond he grew of Southern life with its 'horse-racing, picnicing, boating, fishing, swimming, and God knows what not.' Here he dabbled at painting and dreamed of becoming an artist. He was never more truly happy, and he regretted the War with Mexico that separated him from a social life that he found so 'highly aristocratic and fashionable.' In later years Sherman lived in California, Kansas, and Missouri, not much of a success at any of the several business ventures he tried; and through the intervention of old Southern friends like Braxton Bragg and P. G. T. Beauregard he finally found a niche where he seemed to fit as superintendent of Louisiana's new military college. Here the outbreak of the War Between the States forced his resignation. 'Men are blind and crazy,' he wrote his daughter Minnie, unable to conceal his bitterness.

Sherman's 'nervous-sanguine temperament' seemed ill-suited to military command. Soldiers at first called him 'a hard pill to take' and a 'gruff old cock'; when they knew him better they called him 'Old Sugar Coated.' At one time Sherman was relieved of command, and a Cincinnati newspaper published the story that he was insane, which was giving rather a hard twist to the hallucinations that plagued him; in any event, under the later guidance of other commanding generals, notably Grant, Sherman achieved an emotional stability that permitted him to emerge as one of the great warriors of his age.

Sherman opposed the ruthless carpet-baggers; Johnson, who succeeded Lincoln as President, he described as 'Lear roaring at the wild storm, bareheaded and helpless'; and believing that only 'natural influences' could heal the wounds of war, he said:

> . . . if all hands would stop talking and writing, and let the sun shine and the rains fall for two or three years, we would be nearer reconstruction than we are likely to be with the three and four hundred statesmen trying to legislate amid the prejudices begotten for four centuries.

Compared to the Radicals in Washington, Southerners began to look upon Sherman as a friend, who had opposed the Fifteenth Amendment and who never spared his verbal whip upon what he considered general Republican stupidity in the early post-bellum years. Then in 1875 he published his *Memoirs*. His defense of Confederate General Joseph E. Johnston and his obvious contempt for Jefferson Davis stirred up an anger to equal that at the burning of Columbia. A South on the point of forgiving Sherman began to hate him anew—the more deeply, because now he attempted to destroy Southern sentimentality toward the war. Pride in Southern generalship was the little the South had salvaged from its bloody sacrifices; and Southern tempers bristled as Sherman pictured most of the Confederate generals as neither overbright in private life nor very adept on the battlefield. No Southerner stopped to reflect that under Sherman's harsh scrutiny Northern generalship fared no better: his pen proved far mightier than his sword in bringing down upon his head everlasting enmity and scorn. Fires that burned houses in Georgia and the Carolinas fifty years after the war were blamed on Sherman.

Unhappily, Sherman's voice was one of little influence in the early days of reconstruction. The humiliation, the abuse, the affront to pride and tradition that was heaped upon the South, stupidly and unnecessarily, is caught by Emma. Here is the passion of history—that great motivating force that dominates events and is so difficult to document—which the closing chapters of Emma's diary capture so graphically. Here, clearly revealed, is the rebellious heart that will not be conquered—the spirit fighting to retain its dignity. Whether this impulse of history is right or wrong, just or unjust, reasonable or unreasonable, does not matter: it is a force that exists. It is the nature of human nature at play, under stress, upon the stage of history.

Introduction

The political and emotional disintegration produced by the ending of the world for the Confederacy was reflected in many ways. For John Wilkes Booth the depraved act of assassination seemed the reasonable answer. Edmund Ruffin, who had fired the first shot at Sumter, took his own life after Appomattox. Henry Wirz, the incredible jailer at Andersonville, reclined on a couch, pale and drunk, while he was tried for his crimes. In Washington the government attempted with utter futility to prove that the assassination of Lincoln was part of a fantastic plot, originated by the Confederate government in Richmond and consummated through agents in Canada, to murder Grant and all the members of Lincoln's Cabinet. Neither the North nor South had expected so hard, so cruel, so long a war, and its acid had burned deeply upon the character of the contending brothers.

Under the circumstances, the bitterness with which Emma writes of these days is surely understandable. Living in an uncertain present and contemplating a future even more uncertain, she is surprisingly composed. During these and succeeding months many Columbian families talked of emigrating to the countries in South America, a move the LeContes were reluctant to make. Yet the rule of the carpet-baggers was as fearful as Emma had anticipated; and eventually, Joseph LeConte moved his family to California where a fresh start could give a sense of freedom from prejudices and passions wrought by the war.

*

The diary has been here reproduced exactly as Emma wrote it, although occasionally, for greater clarity, punctuation, capitalization, and paragraphing have been altered. The annotations are those of the editor.

A special note of indebtedness is due Mrs. Ralph B. Shaw of Decatur, Georgia, Emma's granddaughter, who gave permission on behalf of all the grandchildren to publish the present editon of the diary. In a letter to the editor Mrs. Shaw writes of Emma: 'I remember her as a most interesting old lady; even at eighty-two she was alert mentally and physically—still taught a weekly Bible class, remembered her Latin and Math, was a great student, as well as being indefatigable in the matter of crocheting booties and sacques for the five great grandchildren.' When the LeConte family moved to California, Emma remained behind, the young bride of Farish Carter Furman. In the early part of the war Furman, a cadet at the Citadel, had left with his entire class to enlist in the Confederate army, and when the conflict had ended, he resumed his education in Columbia. Young Furman took his bride to live on the family plantation at Scottsboro, near Milledgeville, then the capital of Georgia; here their two children, Katherine Carter and Elizabeth Nisbet, were born. When the girls were about ten and twelve, Mr. Furman died; and to those who read Emma's diary it will be no surprise that she took over the management of the thousand-acre plantation and the education of her young daughters.

The original copy of Emma's diary is one of the more than 2,500,000 items that comprise the Southern Historical Collection of the Library of the University of North Carolina. A generation ago Dr. J. G. de Roulhac Hamilton, a professor of history at Chapel Hill, believed that many valuable sources of Southern history (and especially personal papers and family archives) might be lost forever unless a suitable repository was provided for them. Today, every investigator using the magnificent Southern Historical Collection that has resulted feels an abiding indebtedness to Dr. Hamilton both for his foresight and for the more than thirty years of travel, letter writing, and diligent searching that he devoted to making his dream become this rich reality. Also whoever works with the Collection quickly incurs an obligation to James W. Patton, its director, and to Andrew H. Horn, librarian of the University of North Carolina, for their friendly, never failing assistance.

EARL SCHENCK MIERS

Edison, New Jersey
February, 1957

WHEN THE WORLD ENDED

1

'The Horrible Picture is Constantly before My Mind'

COLUMBIA, SOUTH CAROLINA, DECEMBER 31ST, 1864. The last day of the year—always a gloomy day—doubly so today. Dark leaden clouds cover the sky, and ceaseless pattering rain that has been falling all day. The air is chill and damp, and the morning wind fills one with melancholy. A fit conclusion for such a year—'tis meet, old year, that thou should'st weep for the misfortunes thou has brought our country! And what hope is there to brighten the new year that is coming up? Alas, I cannot look forward to the new year—'My thoughts still cling to the mouldering past.' Yes, the year that is dying has brought us more trouble than any of the other three long dreary years of this fearful struggle. Georgia has been desolated. The resistless flood has swept through that state, leaving but a desert to mark its

track. And now our hateful foes hold Savannah. Noble old
Charleston is at last to be given up. They are preparing to hurl
destruction upon the State they hate most of all, and Sherman
the brute avows his intention of converting South Carolina into
a wilderness. Not one house, he says, shall be left standing, and
his licentious troops—whites and negroes—shall be turned loose
to ravage and violate.

All that is between us and our miserable fate is a handful of
raw militia assembled near Branchville.[1] And yet they say there
is a Providence who fights for those who are struggling for freedom—who are defending their homes, and all that is held dear!
Yet those vandals—those fiends incarnate—are allowed to over-
run our land! Oh, my country! Will I live to see thee subjugated
and enslaved by those Yankees—surely every man and woman
will die first. On every side they threaten—Lee's noble army
alone stands firm. Foreign nations look on our sufferings and
will not help us. Our men are being killed off—boys of sixteen
are conscripted. Speculators and extortioners are starving us. But
is this a time to talk of submission? Now when the Yankees have
deepened and widened the breach by a thousand new atrocities?
A sea rolls between them and us—a sea of blood. Smoking houses,
outraged women, murdered fathers, brothers and husbands for-
bid such a union. Reunion! Great Heavens! How we hate them
with the whole strength and depth of our souls!

I wonder if the new year is to bring us new miseries and suf-

1. Branchville, South Carolina, was 65 miles equidistant from Charleston,
Augusta, and Columbia and was on the strategically important Charleston
and Savannah Railroad. Not until Sherman reached Branchville would he
be forced to disclose in what direction he intended to strike.

ferings. I am afraid so. We used to have bright anticipations of peace and happiness for the new year, but now I dare not look forward. Hope has fled, and in its place remains only a spirit of dogged, sullen resistance.

JANUARY IST, 1865. What a bright new year! If only the sunshine be a presage of happier days! Cold but clear and sunny—such a contrast to yesterday's tears. With this bright sun shining on me I can't feel as mournful as I did yesterday. I will try to throw off the sad memories I was brooding over and hope for better things. I will try to forget my struggles and failures and disappointments and begin again with new resolutions. Oh, me! I haven't much confidence in my ability to keep them!

Yesterday we had a letter from my darling father.[2] He was at Thomasville. He has been gone two weeks, and I suppose by this time he is at the Altamaha. The Gulf Road only runs thus far, and there he will have to stop and get word if possible to Aunt Jane, with Sallie, Cousin Ada, and Cousin Annie to meet him. If that is impossible, he will try to make his way through the lines to them. Though I never say anything about it, I feel uneasy in regard to Father. The Yankees have been through

2. With the news that Sherman had left Atlanta and was marching to the sea, Emma's father worried for the safety of his widowed sister (Aunt Jane), his own fourteen-year-old daughter (Sallie), and his two nieces (Ada and Annie), who were at Halifax, a plantation about thirty-five miles south of Savannah. On December 9th he set out to find these relatives; he returned to Columbia on February 7th. See 'Ware Sherman, A Journal of Three Months' Personal Experience in the Last Days of the Confederacy by Joseph LeConte (Berkeley, 1937), pp. 1-81, hereafter cited as LeConte; and The Autobiography of Joseph LeConte, edited by William Dallam Armes (New York, 1903), chap. VIII.

Liberty County, burning and destroying, and I hear they have passed right through our plantations. Father says, however, that he has heard of no outrages committed. But how dreadfully they must have been frightened. And what is worse, if the provisions have been destroyed, they may be suffering. The uncertainty is very horrible. But how accustomed we have grown to what is horrible!

We had a letter from Grandma, too. She had left us to be with Aunt Sallie in her confinement. She gives a long account of her journey, performed mostly in government wagons with Lee's men. Poor Aunt Sallie suffered dreadfully, and her babe was born dead—the result of the fright she experienced when the enemy passed through Milledgeville.[8]

The old year did not die without bringing us one more piece of bad news. We heard yesterday that Gen. Price—old 'Dad Price[4]—was dead. Misfortunes assail us on every side. The Presi-

---

3. Sherman's troops reached Milledgeville, the capital of Georgia, on November 23. Emaciated Union prisoners from Andersonville caught up with Sherman's forces there, and Yankee tempers grew ugly at the 'wild-animal stare' in the eyes of these bedraggled soldiers. Sherman's avowed policy on these early days of his march was to make war 'so terrible that when peace comes it will *last*.' Moreover, he intended to deal harshly with Georgians, explaining that 'if the enemy burn forage and corn on our route, houses, barns and cotton gins must also be burned to keep them company.' Reports widely published both North and South of a scandalous ball where white officers and Negresses reputedly fraternized licentiously were wholly untrue, and in early January the *Richmond Whig* admitted that the 'Milledgeville myth' should be forgotten. Lloyd Lewis, *Sherman, Fighting Prophet*, New York, 1932, pp. 442–52.

4. Sterling Price. Missouri regiments in Atlanta had heard that guerilla forces, under Price, had invaded their homeland and left a trail of rape behind. When these Missourians struck into Georgia and South Carolina, they boasted openly that they had a score to settle with Price.

dent, however, is quite well again. What a sinking despair I had when I heard that he was dead.

JANUARY 2ND.   Have just returned from Aunt Josie's, where we spent the evening in company with Capt. and Mrs. Green.[5] We had a very pleasant evening and were regaled in honour of the new year, which yesterday being Sunday was celebrated today, with eggnog, Confederate cake and popcorn. Capt. Green of the Nitre Bureau is an odd sort of man, and his wife is awfully ugly. No more news today except that I heard that Jeff Davis said that he would defend Carolina at all hazards. I hope it is true, but I do not believe it.

JANUARY 4TH.   What a budget of bad news this morning! Four letters. One from Father, who writes from camp at Doctortown only fifteen miles from Halifax, but he cannot get there. He had sent word to Aunt Jane by some scouts to try to reach him with the girls, but how can they when every mule and horse has been taken—they could only walk, and that, of course, would be impracticable. Father said the Yanks made a clean sweep of everything, and we have lost all our worldly possessions except the few negroes here. Perhaps Aunt Jane's family and Sallie are almost starving! Oh, it is too dreadful to think of! A second letter from Aunt Ann in Baker County says that Will and Joe Henry (Quarterman), seeing the outrageous conduct of the Yankees in one of the upper counties, mounted and rode night and day to reach Liberty [County] in time to beseech their mother and sisters to run anywhere rather than encounter such

5. Allen J. Green, who commanded the Confederate post at Columbia.

fiends. The house was surrounded (so says report), Willy was killed, Joe Henry mortally wounded, and Gus taken prisoner. Cousin Corinne's husband was found in the swamp. How I hope it is not true! Poor Aunt Harriet! She has so recently buried her husband and daughter. And oh, what are my feelings when I think of Aunt Jane, Annie and Ada and poor little Sallie! What fate may not have overtaken them, alone as they are upon the plantation!

And Father—I cannot bear to think of him. Every day I tremble with the fear that I may hear he is a prisoner or killed. Killed— oh, no—God would not be so cruel as that—I could not think of that—my darling, precious father, if you were only safe at home again! Grandma writes more dreadful accounts of outrages and horrors that happened in Milledgeville. Walter writes from the hospital in Charleston that he has been laid up with chills and fever as a consequence of the terrible march after the evacuation of Savannah. He has got transferred to our College hospital, and we expect to see him this evening.

I am constantly thinking of the time when Columbia will be given up to the enemy. The horrible picture is constantly before my mind. They have promised to show no mercy in this State. Mother wants to send me off, but of course I would not leave her. I can only hope their conduct in a city will not be so shocking as it has been through the country. Yet no doubt the College buildings will be burned, with other public buildings, and we will at least lose our home.

JANUARY 6TH. A horrid day. Rain, rain, rain. I have been sitting over the fire knitting and reading. Mother sitting opposite with her knitting asked me such endless questions in regard to her stocking that I put down my book impatiently and am trying to write. I feel awfully cross and out of sorts, and can't at all understand how so simple an affair as knitting a stocking should appear an insoluble problem. Mother can't conquer the mystery of 'turning the heel'—there it is again—'Emma, how many times did you say I must knit plain?' I think I shall put my pen down and run away.

It was brighter this afternoon in spite of the angry clouds. The sun was setting as we finished dinner and I brought my book out on the piazza where the rosy clouds divided my attention with the pages, when Mother came and asked me to take Carrie.[6] I fear I did so ill-naturedly, but the little darling's laughing face and merry blue eyes soon put me in a better humor, and I raced up and down with her till Jane came, when I ran upstairs, brushed my hair and, coming down again, found the moonlight struggling through the clouds.

JANUARY 10TH. What a day! The rain is sweeping down in torrents and the earth is flooded—not a living creature to be seen—not even a benighted soldier in the campus usually so alive with them. Nothing but the driving rain and rushing water. It is perfectly splendid!

JANUARY 12TH. Last night Cousin Lula and Johnnie came over and we all—Mother, Mr. Memminger—son of Father's old friend,

6. Emma's younger sister Caroline, just past the toddling stage. Among her own most vivid memories of these years in Columbia was her doll: 'he was up in the University museum; he was the skeleton of a man, beautiful beyond comparison and worthy of all affection.' *LeConte*, XVI.

Col. Memminger,[7] and who had been with us for quite a while before Father left, and still seems like a member of the family—Walter, Cousin Lula, and myself, gathered round the table and made 'kiss verses' all the evening for our grand bazaar. As might be supposed, there was lots of nonsense and laughing over our work—if I except Walter, who was as silent as usual. I do not know what is the matter with him—he used to be so very talkative and now he is so gloomy—perhaps it is his health.

Troops have been passing through Columbia for some days and I feel a little safer, though if Joe Johnston[8] is put in command, we had as well pack up and prepare to run. He will certainly execute one of his 'masterly retreats' from the coast back to Virginia, and leave us at Sherman's mercy. I hear that Sherman has drawn his troops back from South Carolina to Savannah. Some think this bodes ill for Gen. Hood,[9] who is in Alabama or Mississippi or somewhere else, and may be caught in a trap

---

7. Christopher Gustavus Memminger, Confederate Secretary of the Treasury. The Memmingers were a remarkable South Carolina family. One of the better stories about them concerned a lady in the family who became an heiress because 'when she was young, an eccentric, rich uncle looked at her nose. "It is so short, she'll never find a husband." So he left her all his fortune in his will, by way of compensation. The better nosed were cut off without a shilling.' Mary Boykin Chesnut, *A Diary from Dixie* (Boston, 1949), p. 385, hereafter cited as *Chesnut*. In April, 1864, Mrs. Chesnut noted: 'The female brigade of Memminger's Treasury Department has been moved to Columbia. That looks squally!' Ibid. 401.

8. General Joseph E. Johnston, who was relieved of command prior to the Battle of Atlanta. Actually, Johnston had handled Confederate forces skillfully in retreating before Sherman's stronger army.

9. John Bell Hood, who replaced Johnston, and after defeat at Atlanta retreated toward Nashville.

between Sherman and Thomas.[10] I hope not. Cousin Lula says they had a letter from Julian yesterday. He, who used to be such an ardent Georgian, is down on the State for behaving so shamefully. He says all his company have abjured their State, and made a vow never to live in it, especially in Savannah. As for me, I am a South Carolinian. I have lived here almost since I can remember, and only wish I had been born here instead of in Georgia! That whole State is utterly demoralized, and ready to go back into the Union. Savannah[11] has gone down on her knees, and humbly begged pardon of Father Abraham, gratefully acknowledging Sherman's clemency in burning and laying waste their State! Oh, it is a crying shame, such poltroonery!

Father writes that he will try to get them all out of Liberty County under a flag of truce. I wish he would make haste and come home—who can tell how soon communication may be cut off.

JANUARY (BETWEEN THE 13TH AND 17TH). We have no more news from Father this morning, indeed there are no mails. The late freshet has carried away the bridges over the Edisto. The

10. George H. Thomas, Virginia-born Union general who won renown as the '*Rock of Chickamauga.*' When after Atlanta Sherman divided his army into two wings—one to march with him to the sea and the other to pursue Hood—Thomas commanded the columns that finally defeated the Confederates before Nashville.

11. Sherman entered this coastal city on December 22nd and telegraphed Lincoln: 'I beg to present you as a Christmas gift the city of Savannah, with one hundred and fifty guns and plenty of ammunition, also about twenty-five thousand bales of cotton.' (38,500 bales actually were seized.) For years afterward Negroes in Savannah dated events from the 'time when Tecumpsey was here.' Earl Schenck Miers, *The General Who Marched to Hell* (New York, 1951), pp. 271-8, hereinafter cited as *Miers.*

Greenville road is so injured that it cannot be repaired under three weeks, and worse still, the Danville road upon which Lee depends for his supplies cannot be used for ten days and he is short of provisions. The very elements conspire against us! Madame D'Ovilliers is going to make us repeat our comedy that came off with so much éclat in the Fall. We rehearse this afternoon.

JANUARY 18TH. Well, our great bazaar opened last night, and such a jam! I was at the State House helping to arrange the tables until four o'clock, so I was thoroughly tired. There are seven booths in the House (of Representatives)—South Carolina, at the Speaker's desk, is the largest, and on either side are Texas, Tennessee, Virginia, Mississippi, Louisiana, and Missouri. In the Senate are North Carolina, at the desk, Arkansas, Georgia, Alabama, and Florida. The tables or booths are tastefully draped with damask and lace curtains, and elaborately decorated with evergreens. To go in there one would scarce believe it was war times. The tables are loaded with fancy articles—brought through the blockade, or manufactured by the ladies. Everything to eat can be had if one can pay the price— cakes, jellies, creams, candies—every kind of sweets abound. A small slice of cake is two dollars—a spoonful of Charlotte Russe five dollars, and other things in proportion. Some beautiful imported wax dolls, not more than twelve inches high, raffled for five hundred dollars, and one very large doll I heard was to raffle for two thousand. 'Why,' as Uncle John [12] says, 'one could

12. Emma's Uncle John was superintendent of the works of the Nitre Bureau in Columbia.

buy a live negro baby for that.' How can people afford to buy toys at such a time as this! However, I suppose speculators can. A small-sized cake at the Tennessee table sold for seventy-five dollars.

The bazaar will continue until Saturday. They had intended holding it for two weeks, but Sherman's proximity forces them to hurry up. I heard, but it is only one of Mr. Johnston's stories, that the aforesaid individual had announced his intention of attending the Ladies' Bazaar in person before it closes.

The railroads are so broken up that we can hear nothing definite, but report says that Sherman is marching one column on Augusta and one on Branchville. One piece of bad news is certain, namely that Fort Fisher[13] has fallen at last.

I had expected to take great interest in the Soldiers' Bazaar, but I cannot. It seems like the dance of death, and who can tell that Sherman may not get the money that was made instead of our sick soldiers. How long before our beautiful little city may be sacked and laid in ashes. Dear Columbia, with its lovely trees and gardens. It is heart-sickening to think of it. Grandpa wants to leave for Georgia as soon as the trains run through, which will be on Friday, and he wants to take me with him, but I think Mother and I had better stay or run together.

We are going to pack up Father's books and as many things as we can and get those of our friends who remain to take care of them as almost any house in the town will be safer than these buildings; then perhaps we may run with Uncle John's family to whatever point he moves the Nitre Bureau works. Oh, it is so

13. Fort Fisher, North Carolina, fell to Federal forces on January 15. It was of vast strategic importance to Sherman, marching northward.

dreadful, and yet how callous our hearts have grown. Two years ago with what despairing agony I would have looked upon the prospect before us, and now I only feel a dull heart pain. If we were anywhere but in this State, it would not be so horrible, but who can tell what will be our fate. Oh, if Father were only at home to advise us what to do. Sometimes I wonder I can be so calm. We have not heard from him in two weeks. He may be in Augusta or Branchville waiting to get through, but if Sherman should reach those places before him and cut him off from us! Oh, this fearful uncertainty is heart-breaking!

JANUARY 21ST. SUNDAY. News from Father and Sallie at last. They are safe, and I am *so* happy. How doubly happy now that I know all that he has endured and escaped. He was a week in the county surrounded by Yankees. He walked 72 miles in three days. Sallie and Cousin Annie and Ada (are to) be sent out by a flag of truce. Poor Sallie gives a dreadful account of her adventures. She walked half the distance to Doctortown, camping out in the woods at night with no shelter, crossing burnt trestles and swollen streams on logs. Poor child! If you were only safe at home again. The nearer the time approaches, the longer and more weary it seems. Father's letter was dated the 9th, Sallie's from Thomasville the 12th, while they awaited a conveyance to take them to Albany. So as soon as the road is repaired, which will be on Tuesday or Wednesday, I shall begin to hope for them. Sallie has been gone nearly three months, and Father five or six weeks.

A new trouble—Walter is down with the measles, and we fear if little Carrie should get them it will kill her in her delicate

=⟨ *14* ⟩=

state of health. Mother is trying very hard to keep her from the infection. Things are looking very gloomy. I heard Gov. Magrath[14] had received orders to hold Charleston, but Mr. Memminger, who was here yesterday, says it is being evacuated. They say Richmond and Petersburg are to be given up, and Lee's army [to] fall back to South Carolina. That would be safer for us, but who could endure the idea of giving up Richmond! Glorious old Richmond, that we have been defending so long—to fall after all those battles—that would be the darkest, darkest day of all.

Everyone seems to feel that Columbia is doomed. Aunt Josie thinks we had all better run off with the Nitre Bureau and camp in the woods of North Carolina till danger is over. They say Sherman is massing his forces at Branchville. Oh, what times to live in! Who knows what may become of us in ten days! Columbia is thought in so much danger that the ladies closed the Bazaar on Friday. Yet all this does not rouse us. We seem sunk in an apathy. Nothing could surprise me now, unless some wonderful help should break in upon our trouble and give us the independence we have been longing and fighting for all these sad years. Even my books fail to keep my attention.

JANUARY 22ND. Mr. Pond has arrived in Columbia with his command. He says Butler's[15] cavalry—five thousand strong—will

14. A.G. Magrath, a former judge of such solid Confederate convictions that his picture had been painted 'tearing off his robes of office in rage and disgust at Lincoln's election.' *Chesnut*, 3.

15. Matthew C. Butler. His brigade was ordered to South Carolina on January 19. *Official Records*, 1, Pt. 2, 1071.

be stationed here for the present, so we will have some security at least from raids. We can hear no news from the army, except that Hood has been relieved of the command at his own desire. Taylor[16] is in command *pro tem.* No one seems to know the whereabouts of either Hood or Thomas. There is talk in Congress of making a commander-in-chief, and some recommend Joe Johnston. Gen. Lee is the only man for that office.

JANUARY 23RD.   No more news from Father. I begin to think he has stayed to get the negroes out. We hear so many rumors of the movements of the Yankees and of our own troops, but they are not worth noting. Mother has packed up the clothing and bed-linen that we may save those at least. All the books are packed, too. I have not been in the library since they were taken down. It would make me too sad to look at the empty shelves.

It may be of interest some day to recall the poor style in which we lived during the war, so I shall make a few notes. My under-clothing is of coarse unbleached homespun, such as we gave the negroes formerly, only much coarser. My stockings I knit my-self, and my shoes are of heavy calfskin. My dresses are two calicoes (the last one bought cost sixteen dollars a yard), a homespun of black and white plaid, and an old delaine of pre-war times that hangs on in a dilapidated condition, a reminiscence of better days. We have a couple of old silks, carefully preserved for great occasions and which do not look shabby for the simple reason that all the other old silks that still survive the war are in the same state of decay. The homespun cost about eight or ten dollars a yard—calico is twenty to thirty dollars a yard now,

16. Richard Taylor, then stationed at Meridian, Mississippi. Ibid.

and going higher from week to week. My shoes are one hundred and fifty dollars a pair. In two or three months these prices will be doubled.

We live tolerably poorly. Two meals a day. Two plates of bread for breakfast, one of wheat flour as five bags of flour were recently made a present to us else we would only have corn bread. Corn itself is forty dollars a bushel. Dinner consists of a very small piece of meat, generally beef, a few potatoes and a dish of hominy and a pone of corn bread. We have no reason to complain, so many families are so much worse off. Many have not tasted meat for months, and we, too, having a cow, are able to have butter. Wood is hard to get at one hundred dollars a load. We keep but one fire in the dining room where we sit. We have been fortunate in having gas thus far (at eighty dollars a thousand), but since the freshet, the supply of rosin has been deficient and now and then it is cut off and we burn tallow candles at two dollars apiece. We never have sweet things now, and even molasses candy is a rarity seldom to be thought of.

2

'What a Panic the Whole Town is in'

JANUARY 25TH. Last night while I was lying on the sofa, feeling very blue and full of gloomy thoughts in regard to the war and the dreadful possibility of the South having to yield, Uncle H. John came in the library and said, 'Well! Have you heard the last report? It is said that England and France conjointly will certainly recognize us by the fourth of March.' I jumped up with the first thrill of real joy I have felt for a long time. A bright vista of peace and happiness seemed to open up before my mind's eye. Of course a moment's reflection sobered me and brought me back to common sense. I recollected with a sigh how often we had been disappointed and lured on to false hopes by that will-o-the-wisp 'Recognition' and 'Intervention,' yet there are some circumstances that lend a slight colouring of possible truth to this rumor. Although at the height of their success, the Yankees are making fair proposals through their Commissioner Blair,[1] if the South will only yield slavery. Dispatches say that much excitement prevails in Richmond, gold has fallen, and the people are selling out. I think I would rather the South were conquered than that she should make peace with them! Father has not come home yet, and we hear nothing. How tired we are of waiting— how I long to see them. Today is Johnny's birthday. He is fifteen. Mother sent him one of our cobwebbed bottles of champagne—a few still lurk in the pantry. I tell Mother she must keep some for *peace* if we ever live to see it.

JANUARY 27TH.   Another day and the long-looked-for have not returned. (Later) We have just received a letter from Sallie. She and Cousins Annie and Ada are in Macon with our relatives (the Clifford Andersons), while Father has returned to attempt to save Aunt Jane by flag of truce. Sallie entreats us to run if there is the slightest danger from Yankees. 'Oh, Mother,' she says, 'I never want to see them again!' Cousin Ada, in a letter to Aunt Josie, gives a sad account of all they suffered and the brutal rudeness of the soldiers. I am so sorry for her. She and Aunt Jane are turned adrift homeless and destitute.

1. Francis Preston Blair, who in 1861 had acted as intermediary for the War Department in trying to persuade Robert E. Lee to take command in the field of Union forces, thought he could secure a negotiated peace. Lincoln, highly skeptical, permitted Blair to go to Richmond. He returned with a note from Jefferson Davis that said he would appoint a commission 'with a view to secure peace to the two countries.' Lincoln flinched, his worst fears confirmed. In reply, he spoke pointedly 'of securing peace to the people of our *one common* country.' Benjamin P. Thomas, *Abraham Lincoln*, (*New York*, 1952), p. 500-501; hereinafter cited as *Thomas*.

JANUARY 28TH.   Grandpa leaves for Macon the day after tomorrow—a Monday. Mother wanted to send me with him but we came to the conclusion we had best not leave home or separate till Father comes. Mr. Memminger was here this evening to bid us goodbye. He places no confidence in rumors of foreign aid. He left early and a few minutes after, Dr. Nat Pratt[2] dropped in and talked more cheerfully. He seems quite confident we will hear tomorrow that an armistice of 60 days has been declared, having learned that Gen. Hampton[3] has received a telegram to that effect. Gen. Lee has been made Generalissimo, and Hood has taken leave of his army. His farewell address is very manly. He shoulders the whole responsibility of his campaign. Says he did his best and failed.

The weather is intensely, fearfully cold. Walter is getting on very well, but is breaking out in boils now. How dreadfully sick I am of this war. Truly we girls, whose lot it is to grow up in these times, are unfortunate! It commenced when I was thirteen, and I am now seventeen and no prospect yet of its ending. No pleasure, no enjoyment—nothing but rigid economy and hard work—nothing but the stern realities of life. These which should come later are made familiar to us at an age when only gladness should surround us. We have only the saddest anticipations and the dread of hardships and cares, when bright

2. N. A. Pratt, chemist at the Nitre and Mining Bureau.

3. Wade Hampton, who had returned to his native South Carolina. Some grumbled that Hampton wouldn't have come home, except for a tiff with Lee, but others remembered Hampton as a hero wounded at Manassas and on the Chickahominy. Hampton's brigade was ordered to South Carolina on January 28. *Official Records*, I, Pt. 2, 1071.

dreams of the future ought to shine on us. I have seen little of the light-heartedness and exuberant joy that people talk about as the natural heritage of youth. It is a hard school to be bred up in and I often wonder if I will ever have my share of fun and happiness. If it had not been for my books, it would, indeed, have been hard to bear. But in them I have lived and found my chief source of pleasure. I would take refuge in them from the sadness all around if it were not for other work to be done. I do all my own sewing now besides helping Mother some. Now that everything is lost, perhaps we will all have to work for a living before long. I would far rather do that and bear much more than submit to the Yankees.

JANUARY 29TH. SUNDAY.   Dr. Gibbes[4] said yesterday he was quite sure of the fact that Alex. Stephens, I. R. Campbell and R. M. T. Hunter[5] had gone to Washington to treat for peace. There is a general feeling throughout the South that we will have peace before long. There have been these national presentiments before, however, and I cannot give much heed to this one. The whole atmosphere is filled with the wildest rumors. It is hard to study in the present state of affairs, and since Father has been away, I have only tried to read again. Yet in the uncertainty of everything I feel more than ever the pressing necessity of gaining an education and that I ought to try to persevere in

4. James G. Gibbes, who later became mayor of Columbia.

5. Alexander H. Stephens of Georgia, Vice President of the Confederacy; John A. Campbell of Alabama and R. M. T. Hunter of Virginia. In so far as they arrived in Washington with another letter from Davis that spoke of 'the two countries,' their mission was predestined to failure. *Thomas,* 501.

working at it. I could not very well study Physics and Latin while Father is away, but I might finish Conic Sections and review some mathematics. All our future is so uncertain. We cannot look beyond the present moment.

JANUARY 31ST. Just a month since I commenced writing—only a month, yet how many changes even in that short time. Grandpa left us yesterday for Georgia. I have just written again to Sallie. She may have left Macon before my letter reaches her, but if not, the poor child will be anxious enough for news from home.

FEBRUARY 1ST. What a delightful day it is. So balmy and delicious. It is almost oppressive in the sunshine and only the bare trees remind one that it is winter. It is one of those luxurious days that we often have in our Southern February, in which the warm sleepy air seems inviting to dreams and every sound has a softened, far-off cadence. Not a breeze is stirring and even animals seem to saunter along dreamily. What a climate would ours be were it not for these cold spells we have now and then. Sunday it was freezing—today it is Spring. I came out on the piazza to read, but fell to thinking instead of just such days two years ago. Cousin Annie was here and how we wandered over the woods and the fields with Jule, sometimes sitting on the brown pine-straw under that great old pine tree by the gurgling spring, talking lazily in the warm sunshine. What a happy pleasant winter it was and how long ago it seems. When shall we three meet again! Never under like circumstances. She is married and Julian in the army fighting for his country. I only am left in the old place.

When the World Ended

We have received a letter from Father at last! Is that not good news? But my poor darling father—what he has suffered! There were no Yankees this time, but he had the elements to contend with and his sufferings were more than the last. It was during those terrible rains and for five days and nights he was on his feet, wet to the skin and sleeping in that condition. He worked like a negro, carrying Aunt Jane's baggage and enduring every kind of fatigue. He crossed the Altamaha when it was so swollen by the freshet that experienced boatmen thought he risked his life. What I dread is that he may yet be sick from the reaction. I reproach myself a thousand times that I have not felt more anxious about my precious father, but, indeed, we had not the slightest thought that he would meet with any obstacle this time. Father said he would be home about the first, so I look for him Friday or Saturday. How *will* I feel when they are all once more safe at home! I think my heart will overflow with joy and thankfulness.

Night. Still more rumors—peace rumors relative to the Blair Mission and our own Commissioners in Washington. I am not hopeful, but everyone around me seems so confident that I cannot help being infected more or less with the general feeling.

FEBRUARY 2ND. THURSDAY. I cannot expect it, yet I do hope the long-watched-for ones will come tonight. It is almost impossible, yet I long for them so. Not only to feel that Father were safe at home—that [would be] a weight off one's heart—but there is another anxiety now—Little Carrie has the measles. Dr. Thomson said so this morning and we are so distressed about it. I am so anxious about my little darling and so sorry Father will find her sick. She has been so well since he left till now.

FEBRUARY 5TH. SUNDAY.   A rainy day, and consequently neither Mother nor I went to Church. Last evening Mrs. Caldwell sent word that her father had seen Dr. LeConte in Macon, and that he bade him tell us he would start home in a few days. I put on my hat and shawl and ran around there to learn something more definite, but Mrs. C. could not even tell me what day her father was in Macon, but only that he said Father looked quite well but sunburnt from exposure. As I returned I stopped to chat with Cousin Lula on the piazza and lingered so long that the rest of my walk home was through the moonlight. It was so lovely and the air so soft and balmy. We cannot think what could detain Father in Macon. Uncle John thinks the train may come through today. If not, Father may take a government wagon from Augusta, in which case we may expect him Tuesday or Wednesday. He may return just in time for us to take a toilsome flight, for the present plan seems to be to run if the Yankees come.

   After the threats uttered in Georgia against this State, it would seem folly to remain. So we propose to accompany the Bureau. Aunt Josie says Uncle John is putting springs in some of the wagons for our accommodation. We are to travel out of the track of the enemy and stop at some little village until Columbia is out of danger, or until it is decided where the Nitre Bureau will be located. We will carry bedding and impress provisions at government prices for the Bureau. This will be quite an expedition—but I so dread leaving home, for I feel I would never see

it again except in ashes. How one grows accustomed to things—
a year ago all this would have made me half crazy with anxiety
and excitement—now it seems natural. We are prepared for the
worst and dare not look even into the immediate future. I cannot
even attempt to picture to myself what may happen in the next
six weeks, or what may be the fate of our dear, beautiful, old
Columbia.

At Church this afternoon Dr. Palmer said that an ambulance
train was to be sent to Branchville and necessary supplies for the
wounded were solicited from the ladies. I stopped at Aunt Josie's,
coming back to see how Johnnie got on with the measles, and
found him up. Uncle John says in a day or two the town will be
flooded with the wounded—that there will not be sufficient
hospital accommodation, and that private houses will have to be
opened to receive them. Alas! The horrors of war are coming
home to us now. Our College hospital has indeed always been
full, and the disabled, limping soldier has grown to be as familiar
as was formerly the festive student in these classic grounds. But
we have never yet been literally surrounded by the wounded,
the dead and dying. Sometimes I still try to get away from the
horrid present by forgetting myself in a book. I have been reading just now Hitchcock's Religion and Geology. I find a good
many ideas there that M. [young Mr. Memminger] in our talks
advanced as his own—sometimes expressed in the identical words.
I think he had very recently read the book. By the way, M. left
Columbia the other day. It is not likely we will ever be thrown
together again. Well, I had a very pleasant time with him while
he was here. He is right clever, has read a good deal, and his
wild theories and still wilder dreams amuse and entertain me.

'What a Panic the Whole Town is in'

FEBRUARY 7TH. TUESDAY. What gloomy weather it is. The rain is flooding down in torrents. I would not mind the pouring rain, but that my imagination pictures Father and the rest exposed to its fury—perhaps in an open government wagon. We hoped for them a little yesterday—would look for them certainly tonight but that we have been so often disappointed. All this continual fear and anxiety have made me realize how intensely I love my dear, precious Father. Walter has just returned from the Medical Board where he went to secure a sick furlough. He will probably be successful. The hospital is to be moved to North Carolina as Columbia is in danger. Our own movements are unsettled, so altogether he prefers going home to southwest Georgia.

FEBRUARY 8TH. WEDNESDAY. Joy—joy! They have come. Last night when I met Father, I think I was perfectly happy— I was standing downstairs in the basement by the fire (Mother and I have moved down there since Carrie's illness), when I heard a step in the hall. 'It is Father,' I thought, then I tried to persuade myself it was only Walter. Then I heard someone descending the stairs. I ran to the door to find my eager hope realized. With a cry of joy I threw myself in Father's arms and clung to him, kissing him. He was wet through—hair and beard were dripping. After a few moments he went back to Aunt Josie's and fetched Sallie over, who received a glad welcome home. Then such talking! But another time I will try to give some account of their adventures. About ten o'clock this morning, Walter having just left us, I went over to Aunt Josie's to see Aunt Jane and Cousin Ada.

FEBRUARY 9TH. I went to Aunt Josie's to return a glove pattern and to carry over some of Aunt Jane's things that were with Sallie's. Found them all well. Father is not well, however. His return to the house, after his open air life, has given him a severe cold. He and Mother agree to let me teach Sallie, both that she may be studying and that I may learn to teach.

FEBRUARY 11TH. SATURDAY. I hardly know where to begin my journal of yesterday, so many things happened. To begin with the morning: while at the breakfast table, Peter came in from Aunt Josie's to tell us that Jule and Cousin Johnnie had just arrived—imagine our surprise! Shortly afterwards Father received an order from Richmond to pack up and move the laboratory to Athens, Ga. For awhile we, of course, supposed we would go also—even now it still seems probable. So here was abundant subject for thought and talk. To think that we should really have to set to work immediately to pack up and leave home was enough to keep our brain active. Returning from my French lesson, I stopped at Aunt Josie's to find her half crazy with delight at having Jule again—and Aunt Jane equally happy but not quite so overcome, while both boys looked as large and natural as life. They had burst into the house about 8 a.m. without a word of warning. Fancy Aunt Josie's joy at seeing her soldier boy after more than a year's absence, during which time his life has been constantly exposed. Julian is not quite so stout as he was a year ago last Christmas—his beard is quite formidable, and altogether he is a very handsome soldier. Cousin Johnny is somewhat changed but looks well. Their battery is to remain here for the present—to be mounted and then to join Hampton.

Father telegraphed Col. St. John[6] to know if he must accompany the laboratory to Athens. He has not yet received an answer, but since he is consulting chemist, he will probably be kept on the line of telegraph, the two laboratories being consolidated under Pratt. Still he may be ordered to Georgia. It is very hard for me to think of leaving home—yet the town is in such danger, and we feel so restless.

FEBRUARY 12TH OR 13TH. Father brought in some news this morning. First and worst, the Yankees are skirmishing at Orangeburg. Second and more encouraging, Gen. Hampton says Sherman *will not* come to Columbia. At all events, we certainly will know in a day or two what he is going to do. Mr. Walker has been taking steps toward boxing up and sending off the Library, but the Governor does not think he can obtain transportation for such a large collection of books.

FEBRUARY 14TH. TUESDAY. What a panic the whole town is in! I have not been out of the house myself, but Father says the intensest excitement prevails on the streets. The Yankees are reported a few miles off on the other side of the river. How strong no one seems to know. It is decided if this be true that we will remain quietly here, Father alone leaving. It is thought Columbia can hardly be taken by a raid as we have the whole of Butler's cavalry here—and if they do, we have to take the consequences. It is true some think Sherman will burn the town, but we can hardly believe that. Besides these buildings, though they are State property, yet the fact that they are used as a hospital

6. Isaac M. St. John, chief of the Nitre and Mining Bureau.

will, it is thought, protect them. I have been hastily making large pockets to wear under my hoopskirt, for they will hardly search our persons. Still, everything of any value is to be packed up to go with Father. I do not feel half so frightened as I thought I would. Perhaps because I cannot realize they are coming. I hope still this is a false report. Maggie Adams and her husband have promised to stay here during Father's absence. She is a Yankee and may be some protection and help. Our sufferings will probably be of short duration, as they will hardly send more than a raid. They would not have time to occupy the town. But I cannot believe they are coming! Aunt Josie and all will remain, I suppose. Indeed, they would not have time now to put into execution their projected flight. Alas, what may we not have gone through with by the end of this week! Ah me, I look forward with terror, and yet with a kind of callousness to their approach.

Night. Father says the above is a false alarm. It was only a raid of 300 men which was repulsed by our forces. The evil day is at least postponed.

FEBRUARY 15TH. WEDNESDAY. Oh, how is it possible to write amid this excitement and confusion! We are too far off to hear and see much down here in the Campus, but they tell me the streets in town are lined with panic-stricken crowds, trying to escape. All is confusion and turmoil. The Government is rapidly moving off stores—all day the trains have been running, whistles blowing and wagons rattling through the streets. All day we have been listening to the booming of cannon—receiving conflicting rumors of the fighting. All day wagons and ambulances have been bringing in the wounded over the muddy streets and through the drizzling rain, with the dark, gloomy clouds overhead.

All day in our own household has confusion reigned, too. The back parlor strewed with clothing, etc., open trunks standing about, while a general feeling of misery and tension pervaded the atmosphere. Everything is to go that can be sent—house linen, blankets, clothing, silver, jewelry—even the wine—everything movable of any value. Hospital flags have been erected at the different gates of the Campus—we hope the fact of our living within the walls may be some protection to us, but I fear not. I feel sure these buildings will be destroyed.

I wish Mother could have sent some furniture to different friends in town, but it is too late now. Aunt Josie has sent her pictures, Uncle John's manuscripts and some clothing to the Roman Catholic priest house on Main Street. Aunt Jane was here a few moments ago and advised Mother as to what things she had better send off. She says Aunt Josie is in a dreadful state of excitement. Neither Mother nor I are much alarmed, though poor Sallie is very much frightened and has been crying hysterically all the morning. I have destroyed most of my papers, but have a lot of letters still that I do not wish to burn, and yet I do not care to have them share the fate of Aunt Jane's and Cousin Ada's in Liberty County, which were read and scattered along the roads. I will try to hide them. One of my bags is filled. The other I will pack tonight.

Henry will stay with us, and vows he will stand by us through thick and thin—I believe he means it, but do not know how he will hold on. It is so cold and we have no wood. The country people will not venture in town lest their horses should be impressed. So we sit shivering and trying to coax a handful of wet pine to burn. Yonder come more wounded—poor fellows—indeed, I can write no more.

Night. Nearer and nearer, clearer and more distinctly sound the cannon—Oh, it is heart-sickening to listen to it! For two or three hours after dinner the cannonade ceased, but for a half an hour past the same sounds, with the roar of musketry, break upon us—frightfully near and sounding above the din of a tumultuous town and above the rattling carts. Just now as I stood on the piazza listening, the reports sounded so frightfully loud and near that I could not help shuddering at each one. And yet there is something exciting—sublime—in a cannonade. But the horrible uncertainty of what is before us! My great fear now is for Father—Oh, if he were only gone—were only safe!

The alarm bell is ringing. Just now when I first heard it clang out, my heart gave a leap, and I thought at once— 'It is the Yankees.' So nervous have I grown that the slightest unusual sound startles me. Of course I knew it was a fire, yet it was with a beating heart I threw open the window to see the western horizon lit up with the glow of flames. Although we are composed, our souls are sick with anxiety. Oh, if Father were only safely off! I try to be hopeful, but if it is true, as it is said, that this is one of Sherman's army corps, what resistance can our handful of troops make? Oh, if Cheatham's[7] corps would only come! Beauregard[8] said he was expecting it in thirteen hours,

7. General Benjamin P. Cheatham

8. General Pierre Gustave Toutant Beauregard, the hero of Sumter, assumed command of all troops in South Carolina on February 16. *Official Records*, I, Pt. 2, 22.

and that was about 2 p.m. They should therefore be here early tomorrow morning—will they come? Oh, if Columbia could only be saved! They surely ought not to give it up without a struggle.

Later. They have passed our first line of breastworks. No firing tonight. Father and Uncle John leave tonight or tomorrow morning.

FEBRUARY 16TH. THURSDAY. How can the terror and excitement of today be described! I feel a little quieter now and seize the opportunity to write a few lines. Last night, or rather early this morning, Father left. After the last lines in my entry last evening, I went downstairs and found in the back parlor with Father a man calling himself Davis.[9] I had heard Father speak of him before. He met him in Georgia while making his way back home with Sallie, and he was very kind to them during that difficult journey. He calls himself a Confederate spy or scout and is an oddity. I only half trust him—he evidently is not what he pretends to be. He says he is a Kentuckian and is both coarse and

9. Emma's father was puzzled by Charles Davis. On February 1st Le-Conte's journal entry read: 'Mr. Davis (so he calls himself) is certainly a queer fellow. This companion whom we have picked up is quick, ready-witted, his senses all awake, observant, and yet *apparently* open and frank. Though so young—only 20, he says—he has evidently seen much of the world and pretends to be a great reader of character. There seems to be something mysterious about him. The young ladies don't know what to make of him. He attracts, yet repels. Sister thinks he is a Yankee spy. *He* says he is a Confederate spy—that he is a Kentuckian, a member of Lewis' Kentucky cavalry brigade—that he fought the Yankees all through Georgia with Wheeler. As we pass along from time to time he points out places of desperate conflict: yonder, under that tree, he killed a Yankee in self-defence; here he made a narrow escape, &c. Whatever he may be, he has taken a great liking to our party and is very kind and efficient.' *LeConte*, p. 75-6.

uneducated, but wonderfully keen and penetrating. He talked a great deal and entertained us by reading our different characters for us. He has taken an unaccountable fancy to Father—as shown by his hunting him up—and he assures him again and again that he will have us protected during the presence of the Yankees here. He claims great influence with the Yankee officers and entire knowledge of the enemy's movements. All the evening he seemed exceedingly uneasy that Father should so long have deferred his departure and very impatient to get him off. He offered to lend him a horse if that would facilitate his leaving. Father is not uneasy, for our authorities assure him that all is right, but I do not like this man's evident anxiety. Can he know more than the generals?

About half-past twelve Father took leave of us. Thus to part! Father starting on an uncertain journey—not knowing whether he may not be captured in his flight, and leaving us to the mercy of the inhuman, beastly Yankees—I think it was the saddest moment of my life. Of course Father feels very anxious about us, and the last words the man Davis said to him were to assure him that he might feel easy about us. I wonder if there is any confidence to be put in what he says! Hardly, I suppose. We said goodbye with heavy hearts and with many presentiments of evil. After Father was gone, I sat up still, talking with Davis. I could not sleep, and besides I wanted to hear that Father was safely off. We asked our guest how he thought Columbia would be treated; he said he would not tell us, it would alarm us too much. Does he really know all he pretends, or is he only guessing? It was three o'clock before I lay down and fell into a disturbed doze which lasted till seven.

Davis stayed and slept on the ground floor, but was gone before we awoke. The breakfast hour passed in comparative calm. About nine o'clock we were sitting in the dining room, having just returned from the piazza where we had been watching a brigade of cavalry passing to the front. 'Wouldn't it be dreadful if they should shell the city?' someone said. 'They would not do that,' replied Mother, 'for they have not demanded its surrender.' Scarcely had the words passed her lips when Jane, the nurse, rushed in crying out that they were shelling. We ran to the front door just in time to hear a shell go whirring past. It fell and exploded not far off. This was so unexpected. I do not know why, but in all my list of anticipated horrors I somehow had not thought of a bombardment. If I had only looked for it, I wouldn't have been so frightened. As it was, for a few minutes I leaned against the door fairly shivering, partly with cold but chiefly from nervous excitement. After listening to them awhile, this wore off and I became accustomed to the shells. Indeed, we were in no immediate danger, for the shells were thrown principally higher up.

They were shelling the town from the Lexington Heights just over the river, and from the campus gate their troops could be seen drawn up on the hilltops. Up the street this morning the government stores were thrown open to the people and there was a general scramble. Our negroes were up there until frightened home by the shells. The shelling was discontinued for an hour or two and then renewed with so much fury that we unanimously resolved to adjourn to the basement and abandon the upper rooms. Sallie and I went up to our rooms to bring down our things. I was standing at my bureau with my arms full when

I heard a loud report. The shell whistled right over my head and exploded. I stood breathless, really expecting to see it fall in the room. When it had passed, I went into the hall and met Sallie, coming from her room, pale and trembling. 'Oh, Emma,' she said, 'this is dreadful!'

We went downstairs—Mother stood in the hall looking very much frightened. 'Did you hear—' 'Yes, indeed'—and at that instant another whistled close overhead. This was growing rather unpleasant and we retreated to the basement without further delay, where we sat listening as they fell, now nearer, and now farther off. Sallie suffered most—she would not be left alone, and would not allow me to go to the outer door to look about, but would call me back in terror.

The firing ceased about dinner time, but as may be imagined, none of us could eat. During the afternoon a rapid cannonade was kept up and I do not think the forces could have been more than half a mile from here. Dr. Thomson says they are only skirmishing. Davis says we have received reinforcements, but he thinks we cannot hold the town as we have given up the strongest position. He was here this morning during the shelling and stood talking to me in the dining room for some time, giving me a picture of the confusion uptown. Our soldiers had opened and plundered some of the stores. He brought me a present of a box of fancy feathers and one or two other little things he had picked up. He says the bridge will be burned and the town evacuated tonight.

10 o'clock p.m.   They are in bed sleeping, or trying to sleep. I don't think I shall attempt it. Davis was here just now to tell us the news—it is kind of him to come so often to keep us posted. I went up to see him—made Henry light the gas and sat talking to him in the hall, while through the open door came the shouts of the soldiery drawn up along the streets ready to march out. Perhaps the Yankees may be in tonight—yet I do not feel as frightened as I thought I would. Dr. Thomson reassures us. He does not think we shall suffer half as much as we imagine. Maggie is not coming. We three will have to tough it out alone. We have moved into the back basement room. I opened the door which gives from our present sleeping room on the back yard just now, and the atmosphere was stifling with gunpowder smoke. After I left Davis and came downstairs awhile ago the gas went out, so I am writing now by the firelight. I suppose it will be several days before we see gas again. Fortunately Mother has a few candles. Henry had to cut down a tree in the yard today for fuel. But I must put by my pencil for tonight. I wonder what another day's entry will be!

3

‘We Look with Horror and Hatred’

FEBRUARY 17TH. FRIDAY. How long is this distress of mind to continue! It is now about eleven o'clock, and the longest morning I ever lived through. I threw myself on the bed late last night, or rather early this morning, without undressing, feeling if I did not take some rest I would be sick. I lay awake a long time in spite of heavy eyelids, listening to the occasional cannon reports, wondering if the shelling would be renewed and thinking of the tumult there was reigning uptown. At last I fell into a heavy sleep. At about six o'clock, while it was still quite dark and all in the room were buried in profound slumber, we were suddenly awakened by a terrific explosion. The house shook—broken windowpanes clattered down, and we all sat up in bed, for a few seconds mute with terror. My first impression on waking was that a shell had struck the house, but as soon as I could collect my senses I knew that no shell could make such a noise. We lit the candle, and Mother sent Jane to inquire of Henry the cause. Of course he did not know.

I went out of doors. The day was beginning to break murkily and the air was still heavy with smoke. All continuing quiet, we concluded that the authorities had blown up some stores before evacuating. Whatever the cause, the effect was to scare us very effectively and to drive away all thought of sleep. We got up an hour later, almost fainting for we had eaten almost nothing the preceding day. I forced myself to eat a little and to drink a half cup of coffee. After breakfast the cannon opened again and so near that every report shook the house. I think it must have been a cannonade to cover our retreat. It did not continue very long.

The negroes all went uptown to see what they could get in the general pillage, for all the shops had been opened and provisions were scattered in all directions. Henry says that in some parts of Main Street corn and flour and sugar cover the ground. An hour or two ago they came running back declaring the Yankees were in town and that our troops were fighting them in the streets. This was not true, for at that time every soldier nearly had left town, but we did not know it then. I had been feeling wretchedly faint and nauseated with every mouthful of food I swallowed, and now I trembled all over and thought I should faint. I knew this would not do, so I lay down awhile and by dint of a little determination got quiet again. Mother is downright sick. She had been quite collected and calm until this news, but now she suddenly lost all self-control and exhibited the most lively terror—indeed, I thought she would grow hysterical. As for Sallie, her fright may be more easily imagined than described. This condition of affairs only lasted about half an hour, but it was dreadful while it did last. As soon as I could, I put on my pockets and nerved myself to meet them, but by and by the firing ceased and all was quiet again.

It was denied that the Yankees had yet crossed the river or even completed their pontoon bridge, and most of the servants returned uptown. They have brought back a considerable quantity of provisions—the negroes are very kind and faithful. They have supplied us with meat and Jane brought Mother some rice and crushed sugar for Carrie, knowing that she had none. How times change! Those whom we have so long fed and cared for now help us. We are intensely eager for every item of news, but of course can only hear through the negroes. A gentleman told us just now that the Mayor had gone forward to surrender the town.

One o'clock p.m. Well, they are here. I was sitting in the back parlor when I heard the shouting of the troops. I was at the front door in a moment. Jane came running and crying, 'Oh, Miss Emma, they've come at last!' She said they were then marching down Main Street, before them flying a panic-stricken crowd of women and children who seemed crazy. As she came along by Aunt Josie's, Miss Mary was at the gate about to run out. 'For God's sake, Miss Mary,' she cried, 'stay where you are.' I suppose she (Miss M.) thought of running to the Convent. I ran upstairs to my bedroom windows just in time to see the U. S. flag run up over the State House. Oh, what a horrid sight! What a degradation! After four long bitter years of bloodshed and hatred, now to float there at last! That hateful symbol of despotism! I do not think I could possibly describe my feelings.

I know I could not look at it. I left the window and went back downstairs to Mother.

In a little while a guard arrived to protect the hospital. They have already fixed a shelter of boards against the wall near the gate—sentinels are stationed and they are cooking their dinner. The wind is very high today and blows their hats around. This is the first sight we have had of these fiends except as prisoners. The sight does not stir up very pleasant feelings in our hearts. We cannot look at them with anything but horror and hatred, loathing and disgust. The troops now in town are a brigade commanded by Col. Stone.[1] Everything is quiet and orderly. Guards have been placed to protect houses, and Sherman has promised not to disturb private property. How relieved and thankful we feel after all our anxiety and distress!

Later. Gen. Sherman has *assured* the Mayor 'that he and all the citizens may sleep as securely and quietly tonight as if under *Confederate rule.* Private property shall be carefully respected. Some public buildings have to be destroyed, but he will wait until tomorrow when the wind shall have entirely subsided. It is said that one or two stragglers from Wheeler's[2] command fired on the flag as it was borne down Main Street on the carriage containing the Mayor, Col. Stone and officers.

FEBRUARY 18TH. SATURDAY AFTERNOON. What a night of horror, misery and agony! It is useless to try to put on paper any idea of it. The recollection is so fearful, yet any attempt to de-

1. George A. Stone, who commanded an Iowa brigade.
2. General Joseph A. Wheeler, whose Confederate cavalry had badgered Sherman's marchers since leaving Atlanta.

scribe it seems to [be] useless. It even makes one sick to think of writing down such scenes—and yet, as I have written thus far, I ought, while it is still fresh, try even imperfectly to give some account of last night. Every incident is now so vividly before me and yet it does not seem real—rather like a fearful dream, or nightmare that still oppresses.

Until dinner time we saw little of the Yankees, except the guard about the Campus, and the officers and men galloping up and down the street. It is true, as I have since learned, that as soon as the bulk of the army entered, the work of pillage began. But we are so far off and so secluded from the rest of the town that we were happily ignorant of it all. I do not know exactly when Sherman [entered], but I should judge about two or between one and two p.m. We could hear their shouts as they surged down Main Street and through the State House, but were too far off to see much of the tumult, nor did we dream what a scene of pillage and terror was being enacted. I hear they found a picture of President Davis in the Capitol, which was set up as a target and shot at amid the jeers of the soldiery. From three o'clock till seven their army was passing down the street by the Campus, to encamp back of us in the woods. Two corps entered town—Howard's and Logan's[3]—one, the diabolical 15th which Sherman has hitherto never permitted to enter a city on account of their vile and desperate character. Slocum's Corps[4] remained over the river, and I suppose Davis'[5] also. The devils as they

3. Generals Oliver Otis Howard and John A. Logan

4. General Henry W. Slocum

5. General Jefferson C. Davis

marched past, looked strong and well clad in dark, dirty-looking blue. The wagon trains were immense.

Night drew on. Of course we did not expect to sleep, but we looked forward to a tolerably tranquil night. Strange as it may seem, we were actually idiotic enought to believe Sherman would keep his word! A *Yankee*—and *Sherman*! It does seem incredible, such credulity, but I suppose we were so anxious to believe him—the lying fiend! I hope retributive justice will find him out one day.

At about seven o'clock I was standing on the back piazza in the third story. Before me the whole southern horizon was lit up by camp fires which dotted the woods. On one side the sky was illuminated by the burning of Gen. Hampton's residence a few miles off in the country, on the other side by some blazing buildings near the river. I had scarcely gone downstairs again when Henry told me there was a fire on Main Street. Sumter Street was brightly lighted by a burning house so near our piazza that we could feel the heat. By the red glare we could watch the wretches walking—generally staggering—back and forth from the camp to the town—shouting—hurrahing—cursing South Carolina—swearing—blaspheming—singing ribald songs and using such obscene language that we were forced to go indoors.

The fire on Main Street was now raging, and we anxiously watched its progress from the upper front windows. In a little while, however, the flames broke forth in every direction. The drunken devils roamed about, setting fire to every house the flames seemed likely to spare. They were fully equipped for the noble work they had in hand. Each soldier was furnished with combustibles compactly put up. They would enter houses and in the presence of helpless women and children, pour turpentine on the beds and set them on fire. Guards were rarely of any assistance—most generally they assisted in the pillaging and firing.

The wretched people rushing from their burning homes were not allowed to keep even the few necessaries they gathered up in their flight—even blankets and food were taken from them and destroyed. The firemen attempted to use their engines, but the hose was cut to pieces and their lives threatened. The wind blew a fearful gale, wafting the flames from house to house with frightful rapidity. By midnight the whole town (except the outskirts) was wrapped in one huge blaze. Still the flames had not approached sufficiently near us to threaten our immediate safety, and for some reason not a single Yankee soldier had entered our house. And now the fire instead of approaching us seemed to recede. Henry said the danger was over and, sick of the dreadful scene, worn out with fatigue and excitement, we went downstairs to our room and tried to rest. I fell into a heavy kind of stupor from which I was presently roused by the bustle about me. Our neighbor, Mrs. Caldwell, and her two sisters stood before the fire wrapped in blankets and weeping. Their home was on fire, and the great sea of flame had again swept down our way to the very Campus walls.

I felt a kind of sickening despair and did not even stir to go and look out. After awhile Jane came in to say that Aunt Josie's house was in flames—then we all went to the front door. My God! What a scene! It was about four o'clock and the State House was one grand conflagration. Imagine night turned into noonday, only with a blazing, scorching glare that was horrible—a copper colored sky across which swept columns of black, rolling smoke glittering with sparks and flying embers, while all around us were falling thickly showers of burning flakes. Everywhere the palpitating blaze walling the streets with solid masses of flames as far as the eye could reach, filling the air with its horrible roar. On every side the crackling and devouring fire, while every instant came the crashing of timbers and the thunder of falling buildings.

A quivering molten ocean seemed to fill the air and sky. The library building opposite us seemed framed by the gushing flames and smoke, while through the windows gleamed the liquid fire. This, we thought, must be Aunt Josie's house. It was the next one, for although hers caught frequently, it was saved. The College buildings caught all along that side, and had the incendiary work continued one half hour longer than it did, they must have gone. All the physicians and nurses were on the roof trying to save the buildings, and the poor wounded inmates, left to themselves, such as could crawled out while those who could not move waited to be burned to death.

The Common opposite the gate was crowded with homeless women and children, a few wrapped in blankets and many shivering in the night air. Such a scene as this with the drunken, fiendish soldiery in their dark uniforms, infuriated, cursing, screaming, exulting in their work, came nearer realizing the material ideal of hell than anything I ever expect to see again. They call themselves 'Sherman's Hellhounds.'

Mother collected together some bedding, clothing and food which Henry carried to the back of the garden and covered them with a hastily ripped-up carpet to protect them from the sparks and flakes of fire. He worked so hard, so faithfully, and tried to

comfort Mother as best he could while she was sobbing and crying at the thought of being left shelterless with a delicate baby.
While this was going on, I stood with Mary Ann at the kitchen
door. She tried to speak hopefully—I could not cry—it was too
horrible. Yet I felt the house must burn. By what miracle it was
saved I cannot think. No effort could be made—no one was on
the roof, which was old and dry, and all the while the sparks
and burning timbers were flying over it like rain. When the few
things she tried to save were moved, Mother took up little Carrie,
who was sleeping unconsciously, and wrapping ourselves in
shawls and blankets, we went to the front door and waited for
the house to catch.

There we stood watching and listening to the roaring and
crashing. It seemed inevitable—they said they would not leave
a house, and what would become of us! I suppose we owe our
final escape to the presence of the Yankee wounded in the hospital. When all seemed in vain, Dr. Thomson went to an officer
and asked if he would see his own soldiers burnt alive. He said
he would save the hospital, and he and his men came to Dr. T's
assistance. Then, too, about this time, even the Yankees seemed
to have grown weary of their horrible work—the signal for the
cessation of the fire—a blast on the bugle—was given, and in
fifteen minutes the flames ceased to spread. By seven o'clock the
last flame had expired.

About six o'clock a crowd of drunken soldiers assaulted the
campus gate and threatened to overpower the guard, swearing
the buildings should not be spared. By great exertions Dr. Thomson found Sherman, and secured a strong guard in time to rescue
the hospital. Mrs. C., who had been to see after her house, now

returned, and sitting down, sobbed convulsively as she told us of the insults she had received from the soldiery engaged in pillaging her home. An officer riding by ordered the men to stop. So broken down and humbled by the terrible experience of the night was she that she cried out, 'Oh, sir, please make them stop! You don't know what I suffered this night.' 'I don't give a damn for your suffering,' he replied, 'but my men have no right to pillage against orders.'

Fortunately—oh, so fortunately for us—the hospital is so strictly guarded that we are unmolested within the walls.

Oh, that long twelve hours! Never surely again will I live through such a night of horrors. The memory of it will haunt me as long as I shall live—it seemed as if the day would never come. The sun arose at last, dim and red through the thick, murky atmosphere. It set last night on a beautiful town full of women and children—it shone dully down this morning on smoking ruins and abject misery.

I do not know how the others felt after the strain of the fearful excitement, but I seemed to sink into a dull apathy. We none seemed to have the energy to talk. After a while breakfast came— a sort of mockery, for no one could eat. After taking a cup of coffee and bathing my face, begrimed with smoke, I felt better and the memory of the night seemed like a frightful dream. I have scarcely slept for three nights, yet my eyes are not heavy.

During the forenoon Aunt Josie and Aunt Jane came over to see how we had fared. We met as after a long separation, and for some seconds no one could speak. Then we exchanged experiences. They were nearer the flames than we, but they had Dr. Carter with them—someone to look to and to help them. Aunt

Josie says the northern side of their house became so heated that no one could remain on that side of the house, and it caught fire three times. Being outside the hospital buildings they were more exposed than we.

Once a number of Yankees rushed in, saying the roof was on fire. Andrew, the negro boy, followed them up, saw them tear up the tin roofing and place lighted combustibles, and after they went down he succeeded in extinguishing the flames. A tolerably faithful guard was some protection to them. The view from their attic windows commands the whole town, and Aunt Josie said it was like one surging ocean of flame. She thought with us that it was more like the mediaeval pictures of hell than anything she had ever imagined. We do not know the extent of the destruction, but we are told that the greater portion of the town is in ashes—perhaps the loveliest town in all our Southern country. This is civilized warfare. This is the way in which the 'cultured' Yankee nation wars upon women and children! Failing with our men in the field, *this* is the way they must conquer! I suppose there was scarcely an able bodied man, except the hospital physicians, in the whole twenty thousand people.[6] It is so easy to burn the homes over the heads of helpless women and children, and turn them with insults and sneers into the streets. One expects these people to lie and steal, but it does seem such an outrage even upon degraded humanity that those who practise such wanton and useless cruelty should call themselves men. It seems to us even a contamination to look at these devils. Think of the degradation of being conquered and ruled by such a

6. Emma exaggerated, but women probably outnumbered the men forty to one at the time Sherman's troops arrived.

people! It seems to me now as if we would choose extermination. I have only had to speak once to one of the blue-coated fiends. I went to the front door to bid Francena and Nellie C. goodbye early this morning, when a soldier came up the steps and asked me who was the Mayor. 'Dr. Goodwyn,' I answered and turned away. 'Do you know his initials?' 'No,' and I shut the door quickly behind me.

The State House, of course, is burned, and they talk of blowing up the new uncompleted granite one, but I do not know if it can be done in its unfinished unroofed condition. We dread tonight. Mother asked Dr. Thomson (who has been very kind about coming in and in keeping us posted) for a guard, but he says it is unnecessary as double guards will be placed throughout the city. Dr. T. says some of the officers feel very much ashamed of last night's work. Their compunctions must have visited them since daylight. The men openly acknowledged that they received orders to burn and plunder before they crossed the river.[7] The drunken scoundrels who tried to force their way into the Campus this morning have been under guard at the gate—several hundred of them—fighting and quarrelling among themselves for sever[al] hours. Poor Father! What will be his state of mind when he hears of all this? The first reports that reach him will be even exag-

---

7. Sherman afterward denied emphatically that the burning of Columbia had been premeditated and said snappishly to disbelieving South Carolinians: 'Your governor is responsible for this. Whoever heard of an evacuated city to be left a depot of liquor for an army to occupy? I found one hundred and twenty casks in one cellar. Your governor, being a lawyer, or a judge, refused to have it destroyed, because it was private property, and now my men have got drunk and have got beyond my control, and this is the result.' *Miers*, 312.

gerated. It is some comfort to us in our uncertainty and anxiety to hope that he may be safe. The explosion last night was [the] accidental blowing up of the Charleston freight depot. There had been powder stored there and it was scattered thickly over the floor. The poor people and negroes went in with torches to search for provisions.

When will these Yankees go that we may breathe freely again! The past three days are more like three weeks. And yet when they are gone we may be worse off with the whole country laid waste and the railroads cut in every direction. Starvation seems to stare us in the face. Our two families have between them a few bushels of corn and a little musty flour. We have no meat, but the negroes give us a little bacon every day.

8 p.m. There has been no firing as yet. All is comparatively quiet. These buildings are surrounded by a heavy guard, and we are told they are distributed throughout the city. All day the devils have been completing their work of plunder, but in the hospital here we have been exempt from this. When I remember how blest we have been, I cannot be too thankful. We have the promise of a quiet night but I dare not trust our hopes—there is no telling what diabolical intentions they may have. Oh, if they were only gone—even to the last straggler! What a load would be lifted from our hearts. We are anxious to learn the fate of our friends, but the little we can gather (except from Aunt Josie and Mrs. Green) is through the negroes, and ours scarcely dare venture uptown. The Yankees plunder the negroes as well as the whites, and I think they are becoming somewhat disgusted with their *friends*. Although the servants seem quite willing, it is difficult to get any work out of them on account of the wild excitement.

Ah, the dreadful excitement—I seem to stand it very well, but it seems to me we must all be ill when it is over. Anxiety, distress, want of rest and food must tell upon us. Mrs. Wilson (Mr. Shand's daughter) with a babe one week old was moved last night from her father's burning house. The Burroughs escaped with only the clothing they wore. Many, many fared similarly. Some tried to save a little food—even this was torn from their hands. I have heard a number of distressing incidents but have not time to write them down. Oh, the sorrow and misery of this unhappy town!

From what I can hear, their chief aim, while taunting helpless women, has been to 'humble their pride'—'Southern pride.' 'Where now,' they would say, 'is all your pride—see what we have brought you to! This is what you get for setting yourselves up as better than other folks.' The women acted with quiet dignity and refused to lower themselves by any retort. Someone told me the following: Some soldiers were pillaging the house of a lady. One asked her if they had not humbled her pride *now*. 'No, indeed,' she said, 'nor can you ever.' 'You *fear* us anyway.' 'No,' she said. 'By G—, but you *shall* fear me,' and he cocked his pistol and put it to her head. 'Are you afraid now?' She folded her arms and, looking him steadily in the eye, said contemptuously, 'No.' He dropped his pistol, and with an exclamation of admiration, left her.

4

===

'The Abomination of Desolation'

FEBRUARY 19TH. SUNDAY. The day has passed quietly as regards the Yankees. About eleven o'clock last night, as everything seemed quiet and Henry intended to sit up, I thought I would follow Mother's example and get some rest. So without taking off my clothes—only loosening them—I lay down and slept soundly all night. I woke at seven much refreshed. Sallie in a few moments opened her eyes and said, 'Oh, Mother, is it already day? I am so glad. I thought the light in the window was the reflection from a fire.' I rose, took off my clothes for the first time in three days, and after bathing and putting on clean clothes, felt like another being.

This morning fresh trouble awaited us. We thought the negroes were going to leave us. While we were on the back piazza, Mary Ann came to us weeping and saying she feared the

Yankees were going to force Henry to go off with them, and, of course, she would have to go with her husband. He did not want to go and would not unless forced. She seemed greatly distressed at the thought of leaving the master and mistress who had supplied the place of father and mother to her, an orphan. The others, Maria and her children, want to go, I think. They have been dressed in their Sunday best all day. Mary Ann, when she came to get dinner, said she could cook two more meals for us anyway. Mother went over to Aunt Josie's to consult her. She advised that, if they left, Mother should get Dr. Thomson to put some sick men in our house to protect it, and we must all move over there as she has two white servants. On her return, however, she talked to Henry, who vows he will never leave us unless dragged away, and he thinks he can avoid them. They are free, however, at present and we ask as little as possible of them—such as cooking our little food and bringing water from the well. The waterworks being destroyed, we have to get water from the Campus well.

If Jane offers to clean up our room, all very well—if not, we do it ourselves. This afternoon I washed the dinner things and put the room to rights. The house is untouched except this one room we live in which I manage to keep neat and clean. This is my first experience in work of this kind and I find it is better than doing nothing. The negroes, when we ask, however, seem quite willing and have given us not the slightest impertinence.

While Mother was at Aunt Josie's, I took Carrie up in the drawing room to amuse her. While we stood by the front window the house was shaken by a terrible explosion. As the gas works were burning at the time, I concluded it was the gasometer, but remembering we had had no gas for two or three days, that seemed impossible. Henry has just explained it. Our men had buried a number of shells near the river, an attempt was made to excavate them, and one going off accidentally exploded the rest, killing [and] wounding a great many Yankees.[1] How I rejoice to think of any of them being killed. Dr. Bell says about 200 were burnt up Friday night[2]—drunk, perhaps—if only the whole army could have been roasted alive!

The provost guard is encamped opposite the Campus. It consists of one battalion and is to remain until the last straggler leaves the town. Two of the officers went to Aunt Josie's and, saying they wished quarters opposite their camp, she was obliged to accommodate them and give up her library for their use. Their horrid old gridiron of a flag is flaunting its bars in our faces all day. Ever since dark thick clouds of smoke have been rolling up from the arsenal and I fear the flames will spread over the hill. Mary Ann came to see us in great distress this afternoon

1. 'During the 18th and 19th,' Sherman said, 'we remained in Columbia, General Howard's troops engaged in tearing up and destroying the railroad, back toward the Wateree, while a strong detail, under the immediate supervision of Colonel O. M. Poe, United States Engineer, destroyed the State Arsenal, which was found to be well supplied with shot, shell, and ammunition. These were hauled in wagons to the Saluda River . . . and emptied into deep water, causing a very serious accident by the bursting of a percussion shell, as it struck another on the margin of the water. The flame followed back a train of powder which had sifted out, killing sixteen men and destroying several wagons and teams of mules. We also destroyed several valuable foundries and the factory of Confederate money. . . . There was also found an immense quantity of money, in various stages of manufacture, which our men spent and gambled with in the most lavish manner.' William T. Sherman, *Memoirs* (New York, 1875), II, 287-8.

2. This report was fictitious.

to tell us that a Yankee had sworn to her that these buildings should be burned tonight. Enquiring of an officer, Mother was assured there was no danger—I suppose it was only a drunken threat.

Mother looked over the town this morning from Aunt Josie's attic window. She described a scene of fearful desolation. Here all is hidden from us. When they are gone, I will walk out of the Campus and see it all—yet how I dread it! Poor Columbia! Sometimes I try to picture it to myself as it now is, but I cannot. I always see the leafy streets and lovely gardens—the familiar houses. I cannot imagine the ruins and ashes to save my life. *How* I *hate* the people who have done this!

A few moments ago there was a violent ring at the bell. I was the only person awake, and I roused Jane up and sent her upstairs. It was some Yankee officers who wished to know where Mayor Goodwyn lived. Sherman, it seems, wished to appoint a meeting with him in order to leave arms for the citizens to protect themselves from stragglers.[3]

FEBRUARY 20TH. MONDAY. Quite early this morning a Yankee entered the yard looking for Henry, who forthwith locked himself in his room. Mother went out and asked the mean filthy devil if he wished to make Henry go against his will. He hesitated a little, and said, 'No,' but he wished to see him. The soldier—the dirtiest, meanest looking creature imaginable—told

---

3. Sherman's testimony was that he gave the mayor one hundred muskets 'with which to arm a guard to maintain order after we should leave the neighborhood.' Ibid. 287.

Mother, when she threatened to send for the guard if he did not leave, that *he* was one of the guard himself. 'Well,' said Mother, 'there are two officers at my sister's house and I will send to them.' The Yankee turned and left the yard.

Mrs. Bell tells us that Sherman turned loose upon us a brigade that he had never allowed to enter any other city on account of their desperate and villainous character. And yet they talk now of being ashamed of what followed, and try to lay it on the whiskey they found! Shortly after breakfast—oh, joyful sight— the two corps encamped behind the Campus back of us marched by with all their immense wagon trains on their way from Columbia. They tell us all will be gone by tomorrow evening. Oh, that we were completely rid of them! And that Father were with us! I might then know what it is to feel happy one moment. Under other circumstances it would have been a wonderful sight to see this great army with its endless trains march by. With the memory of Friday night burned in, it was hard to look at them.

A great drove of lean, ill-looking cattle was driven into the Campus today—our two cows have not been taken from us. Neither the Roman Catholic, Trinity (Episcopal) nor Presbyterian Churches were burnt. It was a miracle the latter was saved—everything around it was destroyed. In Trinity churchyard soldiers were encamped. Of course there was no Service in any of the churches yesterday—no church bells ringing—the Yankees riding up and down the streets—the provost guard putting up their camp—there was nothing to suggest Sunday. What balmy, delicious weather we have had for three days past— most fortunate it is or there would have been even more suffering. Henry has already cut down two trees in the yard to give us fuel.

Mother has just this moment returned from Aunt Josie's bringing the news that the last of the army is leaving the city. The provost guard has broken up camp also. This leaves the terror of stragglers before us—we expected the guard would remain a day or two. There is no knowing what outrages may be committed. Mother is going to try to get Dr. Thomson to stay here at night. She wants to send me to Aunt Josie's, but I will not leave her alone. We must trust to Henry's protection.

FEBRUARY 21ST. TUESDAY.   The night with its fear of stragglers is past and we may breathe more freely but not less sadly. The destruction and desolation around us which we could not feel while under such excitement and fear now exerts its full sway. Sad? The very air is fraught with sadness and silence. The few noises that break the stillness seem melancholy and the sun does not seem to shine as brightly, seeming to be dimmed by the sight of so much misery. I was at Aunt Josie's this morning and there learned for the first time the extent of suffering. Oh, God! When we think of what we have escaped and how almost miraculously we have been saved we should never rise from our knees. There is not a house, I believe, in Columbia that has not been pillaged—those that the flames spared were entered by brutal soldiery and everything wantonly destroyed. The streets were filled with terrified women and children who were offered every insult and indignity short of personal outrage—they were allowed to save nothing but what clothes they wore, and there is now great suffering for food. It would be impossible to describe or even to conceive the pandemonium and horror. There is no shadow of doubt that the town was burned by Sherman's order. All through Georgia, it is said, he promised his men full license in South Carolina. The signals both for firing and ceasing were given—the soldiers were provided with the materials for the work—and yet I hear that he already denies it and tries to put the responsibility on Gen. Hampton.[4] At one time Friday night, when Aunt Josie's house and other buildings were taking fire, the College buildings were given up and the poor wounded soldiers who could not be moved resigned themselves to death.

Dr. Carter says it was a touching sight to see the poor fellows trying manfully to nerve themselves to meet their fate. And there was the regiment ostensibly sent to extinguish the fire, calmly looking on without raising a finger, and the patriots on the streets themselves applying the torch. The hospital was saved by one Yankee captain and two men, yet it contained many of their own wounded soldiers. The unfinished granite state house was not blown up because they were short of powder and it is unroofed. All that could be destroyed was ruined by the burn-

---

4. Sherman confessed: 'In my official report of this conflagration, I distinctly charged it to General Wade Hampton, and confess I did so pointedly, to shake the faith of his people in him, for he was in my opinion a braggart, and professed to be the special champion of South Carolina.' Ibid. 287. Hampton retorted to this charge in a blaze of indignation through a letter to the editor of the *New York Day Book*. Thundered the angry Hampton, in part: 'Wherever he [Sherman] has taken his army in this State, women have been insulted or outraged, old men have been hung to extort from them hidden treasure. The fruits of the earth have been destroyed, leaving starvation where plenty once reigned, and the dwellings of rich and poor alike have been laid in ashes. For these deeds history will brand him as a robber and incendiary and will deservedly "damn him to everlasting fame." *Miers*, 314-16.

ing of the work sheds—fine carving, capitals, columns, ornamental work, etc. I can hardly help feeling that our total exemption from insult and plunder was due in some way to the influence of the strange man who called himself Davis and promised us protection. Why, in many houses the very guards stationed to protect helped the soldiers in smashing and destroying. It is sickening to listen to the tale of distress, much more to try to write of it. A heavy curse has fallen on this town—from a beautiful bustling city it is turned into a desert.

How desolated and dreary we feel—how completely cut off from the world. No longer the shrill whistle of engine—no daily mail—the morning brings no paper with news from outside—there are no lights—no going to and fro. It is as if a city in the midst of business and activity were suddenly smitten with some appalling curse. One feels awed if by chance the dreary stillness is broken by a laugh or too loud a voice. How unhappy poor Father and Uncle John, Julian and Cousin Johnny will be when they hear of this. There has even been a report afloat that Aunt Josie's house was burned and Cousin Lula perished in the flames—if they should hear that!

I wonder if the vengeance of heaven will not pursue such fiends! Before they came here, I thought I hated them as much as was possible—now I know there are no limits to the feeling of hatred.

FEBRUARY 22ND. WEDNESDAY. I meant last night to write down some description of what I had seen, but was too wretchedly depressed and miserable to even think of it. This morning we have heard that he [Father] is safe and I can take up my journal again. Yesterday afternoon we walked all over the town in company with Miss Ellen LaBorde. Yes, I have seen it all—I have seen the 'Abomination of Desolation.' It is even worse than I thought. The place is literally in ruins.[5] The entire heart of the city is in ashes—only the outer edges remain. On the whole length of Sumter Street not one house beyond the first block after the Campus is standing, except the brick house of Mr. Mordecai. Standing in the center of the town, as far as the eye can reach, nothing is to be seen but heaps of rubbish, tall dreary chimneys and shattered brick walls, while 'in the hollow windows, dreary horror's sitting.' Poor old Columbia—where is all her beauty, so admired by strangers, so loved by her children! She can only excite the pity of the former and the tears of the latter. I hear several Yankee officers remarked to some citizens on the loveliness of their town as they first saw it by sunrise across the river.

Blanding Street, crossing Main and Sumter at right angles, the finest street in town, is also a sad picture. The Preston house, with its whole square of beautiful gardens, escaped. It was Gen. Logan's headquarters. The Crawford house, the Bryce's, the Howe's and one or two others also escaped. All nearer Main Street were burned. The Clarkson house is a heap of brick with most of its tall columns standing, blackened by the smoke. Bedell's lovely little house is in ruins while, as if in mockery, the shrubbery is not even scorched. But I cannot particularize— with *very* few exceptions all our friends are homeless. We enter Main Street—since the war in crowd and bustle it has rivalled a city thoroughfare—what desolation! Everything has vanished as by

5. Reliable estimates place the area destroyed at 366 acres, the number of residences and stores ruined at 1,386.

=⟨ *61* ⟩=

enchantment—stores, merchants, customers, all the eager faces gone—only three or four dismal-looking people to be seen picking their way over heaps of rubbish, brick and timbers. The wind moans among the bleak chimneys and whistles through the gaping windows of some hotel or warehouse. The market [is] a ruined shell supported by crumbling arches, its spire fallen in and with it the old town clock whose familiar stroke we miss so much.

After trying to distinguish localities and hunting for familiar buildings, we turned to Arsenal Hill. Here things looked more natural. The Arsenal was destroyed, but comparatively few dwellings. Also the Park and its surroundings looked familiar. As we passed the old State House going back, I paused to gaze on the ruins—only the foundations and chimneys—and to recall the brilliant scene enacted there one short month ago. And I compared that scene with its beauty, gayety and festivity—the halls so elaborately decorated, the surging throng—with this. I reached home sad at heart and full of all I had seen. Presently we heard a commotion in the yard. Running out on the back veranda we saw, standing in the middle of the yard, Sandy and the boys and the negroes who had remained grouped around them. As soon as they saw us, Annie screamed: 'The Yankees has caught 'em. Mass Johnny's come back and Master's took prisoner.' Asking Sandy about Father, he said that he and Capt. Green were in the woods when the party was captured. We could learn nothing succinct from him, and all tired as we were, rushed over to see Johnny. We found him in the kitchen with Cousin Lula and the two white servants. All the rest were out.

Johnny gave us a description of their capture. The Yankees

they fell in with treated them kindly and he thought Uncle John would soon be paroled. He thought Father must have been captured, as the woods were alive with Yankees. He did not see how they could escape, and he feared he would fare worse for trying to escape. And even if he did escape, the country had been so entirely swept that he could get nothing to eat. Father and Capt. Green were out scouting when the wagons were taken. As Johnny started home yesterday and had seen Father last on Sunday morning, there seemed little grounds to hope that he had not been taken. Yet if I had been certain of his capture, it would have been less dreadful than the thought of his hiding in the woods, cold and hungry, and [with] the possibility of being shot.

It was dreadful—everything was burst open—all our silver and valuables stolen—articles of clothing slashed up by bayonets and burned, with Father's valuable books carried off for safety, and all our table linen and bedding, blankets, etc. But we did not once think of those things in the great anxiety and distress about Father. Then Aunt Josie and Aunt Jane, Mrs. Green and Cousin Ada came in. Cousin Lula went to break the news. Aunt Josie was quite overcome—she and Mother wept together, Aunt Jane trying to comfort them. I drew back in the shadow of the staircase—it seemed as if my heart would break, and I cried by myself till Cousin Ada, turning, said 'poor Emma,' and put her arms around me. It was dark and we had to go home. I rushed upstairs to my room and threw myself down beside the bed—my heart was bursting—one horrible picture always before my eyes.

This morning Mother learned from Moultrie Gibbes that Father is safe. He saw him at a house eighteen miles from Columbia. It is impossible to tell of the relief after such suspense. I feel so thankful. We learned from Sandy that the negroes at the nitre plantation, who were along, have taken possession of, and brought home, some of our things. Mother and Aunt Josie went to Capt. Stanley of the provost guard and he has promised to institute a thorough search for them. But how could we guess that our house would not be treated like the rest? Luckily we did not send off our summer clothing. Sandy says they dived immediately into the box of wine and told him to tell his mistress they were much obliged, as they swallowed hock and champagne.

Henry says one mill has been spared and we can get corn ground. The negroes are flocking in from the devastated country to be fed. Mayor Goodwyn has ordered them to be sent back, as the town is threatened with starvation. Indeed, I do not know what will become of us unless relief comes in, from Edgefield or Augusta. In every other direction we understand the country is a desert—Orangeburg, Winnsboro', Chester, Camden—all in ashes. Incarnate fiends! And Sherman! 'O for a tongue to curse the slave.'

FEBRUARY 23RD. The days are now as monotonous as possible. I do not leave the house. Yesterday, except the portion spent in writing this record, was spent in wandering aimlessly about the house or sitting listless in the sun. This morning I felt I must not be so idle. I tried to read a volume of Madame de Stael 'De la Literature'—it was impossible. I tried something lighter—one of Dickens. I soon found I did not know what I was reading. I thought of commencing a pair of gloves I have been meaning to make for Father—the very thought seemed to make me weary.

'The Abomination of Desolation'

I suppose it is the reaction from the frightful strain and nervous tension—the violent excitement. And then the uncertainty of the future—what is to become of us. If Father would only come home, if we could only leave this desolate place. Sometimes I feel a restless impatience to know what is going on in the world from which we are cut off, and I feel at times an entire and apathetic indifference as to what should transpire.

Mother saw Mr. Gibbes yesterday herself. He said he was passing a house and, hearing some Confederate officers were within, he desired to see them. Whereupon Father and Capt. Green made their appearance at the door, the former with a cup of coffee in his hand. At that time he was expecting to make his way to Winnsboro', but Mr. G. told him the Yankees were gone in that direction and advised him to remain where he was until he heard from Columbia. I looked for him last night and sometimes I fear he may have been caught by Kilpatrick's[6] raiders, but I think I have no reasonable ground for such a fear. There is nothing to do but try to be patient. Patience! How the heavy days creep by! Oh, to see our dear father again after all that has been gone through and suffered since we parted. Dr. Carter left for Augusta this morning and we sent letters by him to Georgia. I wrote a few pages to Cousin Ella—would have written to Cousin Annie but do not know where she is. Mother wrote to Grandmother; I hope the letters will be legible enough when they reach their destination to relieve anxiety. There is not one drop of ink in the house and for ten days I have written this diary in pencil. I wish I could get letters.

6. General Judson Kilpatrick

Sallie has commenced studying and will recite her lessons to me tomorrow. I cannot summon energy or interest to go back to my own studies. That must not be until, anxiety banished, we are reunited and settled down in quiet. When will that be! The Yankees talk very strongly of conquering the South immediately—if so, our day of rest is far off. Somehow I am still as confident as I ever was. If only our people will be steadfast. The more we suffer, the more we should be willing to undergo rather than submit. Somehow I cannot feel we can be conquered. We have lost everything, but if all this—negroes, property—all could be given back a hundredfold, I would not be willing to go back to them. I would rather endure any poverty than live under Yankee rule. I would rather far have France or any other country for a mistress—anything but live as one nation with *Yankees*—that word in my mind is a synonym for *all* that is *mean*, despicable and abhorrent.

I hope relief will come before famine actually threatens. We have to cut our rations as short as possible to try to make the food hold out till succor comes. Father left us with some moldy, spoiled flour that was turned over to him by the Bureau. We can only possibly eat it made into batter-cakes and then it is horrid. We draw rations from the town every day—a tiny bit of rancid salt pork and a pint of meal.[7] We have the battercakes for breakfast, the bit of meat and cornbread for dinner—no supper. We fare better than some because we have the cows.

7. Five hundred head of cattle were left by Sherman to help feed the stricken people; the animals were described as 'overaged and underfed' and reportedly were 'dying of exhaustion' at the rate of fifteen or twenty head a day.

Mother had peas to feed them, and sometimes we take a few of these from them to vary our diet. Today as a *great treat* Mother gave us boiled *rice* for dinner—some the negroes had brought us in the pillage of the stores. We enjoyed it immensely—the first I have tasted in many days.

FEBRUARY 26TH. SUNDAY NIGHT. At last I have something joyful to chronicle—*Father is returned!* Friday evening, as we all sat in the library, there was a knocking at the door, then a violent ring at the bell—we knew what it meant. I rushed to the door first and opened it to fall in Father's arms. What a scene! Embraces, kisses, weeping—he was wet through and in rags. We hurried him to the fire and listened to the story of his escape, an escape that seemed little short of miraculous.[8] I am so thankful and happy every moment that I remember he is safe at home.

Father describes Sherman's track up there as the same it was in the lower part of the State—desolation and ruin. Every night the entire horizon was illuminated by burning houses! Poor Carolina!! And the burning of Columbia was the most diabolical act of all the barbarous war. Father grits his teeth every time he sees the ruins or speaks of the horrors of that night. As far

---

8. Emma's father tells a rousing tale of escape. Trapped in a woods, surrounded by Yankees, he was helped by his Negroes. Once, crawling on hands and knees, he thought: 'How often have I practiced this mode of progression in duck and turkey hunting—now I am the quarry!' On another occasion fatigue so overcame Captain Green that he fell asleep while still walking and was rudely awakened by tumbling into a deep ditch. Both men quickly learned that

In the dark imagining some fear

How easy is a bush supposed a bear.

LeConte, 91-132

as I can see, the people are undemoralized and more determined than ever. The Yankee officers while here paid the tribute to the women of this State of saying they were the most firm, obstinate and ultra-rebel set of women they had encountered—if the men only prove equally so! Father and I went to church this morning. We had a mournful looking congregation. Dr. Howe officiated, reading the first chapter of Lamentations. After church we stopped at Aunt Josie's, who kindly lent us some table silver. All Mother saved was three forks, two tablespoons and two teaspoons which she kept for our use.

Today is Father's birthday.

FEBRUARY 28TH. TUESDAY.   I am now fairly launched as a school-ma'am. I fancy I get on pretty well considering my lack of experience. I teach Sallie arithmetic, Latin, spelling and elementary natural philosophy besides reading and composition. I will begin study myself when Father returns from a trip down the river with Capt. Green to get provisions for the town in general and our two families in particular. They propose starting tomorrow.

Cousin Ada and I went to call on Mrs. Carroll yesterday but found she is not in town, having run away just before the advent of the Yankees! It is not far from her house to the cemetery, so we went there to look at little Josie's grave. Coming home we walked down Main Street—slowly in the middle of the street for fear of falling walls—trying to conjure up the well-known shops and buildings from the shapeless heaps. At the market place we saw the old bell—'Secessia'—that had rung out every state as it seceded, lying half-buried in the earth and reminding me of Retzsch's last outline in 'The Song of the Bell,' showing 'That all things earthly disappear.'

We walked through the State House yard and examined the marks of the shells on the new Capitol. Large pieces of granite are sometimes broken off. On one end alone we counted places where eight shells had struck and exploded.[9] We have since heard that in the accidental explosion of the Charleston freight depot, from the igniting of powder strewn upon the floor, one hundred and fifty or two hundred people were killed.

9. Three stars have been imbedded in the side of the State House to mark where the shells from the Federal cannon struck. Before the building stands a statue of George Washington to which the following tablet in bronze has been affixed:

> DURING THE OCCUPATION OF
> COLUMBIA BY SHERMAN'S ARMY
> FEBRUARY 17-19, 1865
> SOLDIERS BRICKBATTED THIS
> STATUE AND BROKE OFF THE
> LOWER PART OF THE
> WALKING CANE

5

'Hurrah! Old Abe Lincoln has been Assassinated!'

MARCH 1ST. WEDNESDAY. The first day of Spring! A gloomy opening of the bright season. It is not cold, but dark and rainy. Father has been obliged to defer his trip on account of the weather and is waiting for a fair day.

There was a rumor afloat yesterday that a *negro* regiment was marching from Branchville to garrison Columbia. Heavens! Have we not suffered enough? I do not believe it, but the very thought is enough to make one shudder. If Father succeeds in laying in a supply of food, we will probably remain here, unless Father is ordered away.

Communication will soon be opened with Augusta and other towns and probably with Col. St. John. As long as we stay here,

[handwritten margin note: WHAT?]

we have the comforts of home and are among friends. Then if the government works are moved back, I might get some kind of employment.

MARCH 2ND. It still continues damp and cloudy with no immediate prospect of a favorable change. I have not gone back to study but feel heartily ashamed of myself for not doing so. I have resolved not to be idle any longer, but to go back to my books and take up again some solid reading I had planned before all this excitement. This afternoon Father called me downstairs to help him rearrange the books. They had been packed in boxes before the Yankees came, for removal, but Father, finding it impossible to take them off, judged they would be safer in the cases as the soldiers would tumble them out in search of valuables, so just before he left, he had Henry put them back. Of course he placed them on the shelves pell-mell without any regard to order.

I had a good laugh today with Sallie. I mentioned in my account of the shelling of the town on Thursday that the man Davis brought me a box of feathers. I had laid them away and did not think of them till today, when I came across them and we were looking over them, selecting some that I thought would make a pretty fan. Near the bottom of the box Sallie spied a folded paper, a leaf from some notebook. She opened it. At the top of the page was a rude drawing of two hearts—this, the note said, 'portrayed two hearts surrounded by rosebuds' (the rosebuds being entirely imaginary). 'May they (continued the note) prove an emblem of our hearts, may they be joined by the golden links of friendship and may the rosebuds of life entwine them and though many hundred miles separate us may we be always firm friends.'

Well, if that individual is not a queer fish I never met one! He was [a] pretty rough specimen, but if we owe anything to his kindness of heart, I ought not to be too hard on his coarseness. Of course Sallie got a lot of fun out of it, showing it in high glee to Father, who was greatly amused over it. The fellow had remarkable keen insight into character. The evening he talked with me after Father was gone he hit off his character wonderfully except in one or two points—remarkable, considering how absolutely Father differed from himself. He read both Mother's and my character too. Mine, except for the flattery he threw in, was very correct also.

MARCH 7TH. TUESDAY. Last Friday (3rd) we received two pieces of good news. In the first place Dr. Pratt arrived with four wagons to our relief. Two hours after receiving Father's letter he started. In that short time provisions were hastily collected and clothing for Father, Uncle John and Capt. Green (Father has been wearing a pair of blue trousers taken from a dead Yankee soldier at the hospital and given him by one of the doctors).

The officers of the Nitre Bureau contributed, throwing in shirts, collars, socks, etc. When he got to Prof. Holmes[1] in Edgefield that generous-hearted friend set to work and loaded up a wagon with bacon, corn, clothing, etc., and sent word we must all come to his home right away. Such friends in times like

1. E. S. Holmes, superintendent of Nitre and Mining District No. 6, South Carolina

these of scarcity and selfishness are indeed to be appreciated. Dr. Pratt left so hurriedly that he did not even go home to bid his wife goodbye—only despatched her a note. He says no one in Augusta has the slightest conception of the desolation here; they suppose that only Main Street was burned, and that, the Yankees said, was done accidentally by our own soldiers in destroying cotton! As soon as the state of things was better understood, contributions poured in. Our necessities are supplied for the present and we need not now draw rations from the town as we have been doing ever since the fire.

The Mayor issues rations to 7,000 people—all that is left of a population of about 30,000. The original population of 12,000 was enormously increased since the war by refugees and other sources.

The other piece of good news was received last night—that Uncle John was paroled in Chester. Aunt Josie's joy was unbounded and her excitement brought on a severe attack of palpitation of the heart. Last evening she received a letter from him. He is within twenty-seven miles of Columbia, but is waiting to get a conveyance. One of his feet is so sore from making a march of fifty miles with the Yankees that he cannot walk it. Chester was not burned. The Yankees did not go either there or to Yorkville. The greater part of Winnsboro' was destroyed and the whole of Lexington—in fact, every town and village in their track.

Prof. Pratt stayed with us while here. Father, giving up his expedition down the river, returned with him to Augusta yesterday to see what he could do about getting supplies from there. We expect him back in one or two days. We can hear nothing

=⟨ 74 ⟩=

from our army. For the first time we are without the excitement of daily telegraphic news and I miss the breakfast table discussions of the war news and the movements of the forces. We live in absolute ignorance while our fate is being decided, and speedy peace and long-continued war are trembling in the balance. At all events we miss perhaps a thousand unfounded and conflicting rumors. We are hoping for intervention, but that may mean humiliating concessions. If recognition meant the opening of our ports only, that would be all we would ask. Once freely supplied with materials for war we would soon be independent. That is all we need.

MARCH 8TH. WEDNESDAY. Uncle John got home last night. It has been raining all day and I have not been to see him. He is confined to the house with his foot.

I am back at my books again and read a great deal. I do nothing else, except, of course, knitting, which does not interfere at all with my reading. I have gone at old Gibbon again and mean to finish him. Am also reading Hitchcock—especially in the metaphysical portions of the latter I need Father so much. I hope he will not have to go off again. I do want to get steadily and systematically at work again.

MARCH 10TH. FRIDAY. Today is the day of fasting and prayer appointed by the President. It rained so hard all the morning, however, that none of us went to church. Even if the weather were favorable I could not go as I am not at all well, nor have been for several days, but only began to feel like giving up yesterday. Nevertheless I went, in spite of threatening clouds, to see Uncle John in the afternoon. He had a hard time with the Yankees—was not allowed a blanket to sleep on—no fire, and had to march over a hundred miles with them. He saw one of his own negroes, Peter, on horseback while he was plodding on foot. On the whole, though, he looks very well and feels more like himself except for his foot. Aunt Josie was sick in bed. Uncle John said that while he was marching along a Yankee officer rode beside him and asked, 'What will you Southerners do when we have marched victoriously through Virginia and taken Richmond?' 'I think Gen. Lee may have something to say to that,' he replied. 'You have him to meet yet.' 'Well, suppose we defeat and disperse his army?' 'I suppose then we will have to resort to guerilla warfare.' The officer looked surprised and shocked. 'Why cannot you yield?' he asked. Uncle John shrugged his shoulders and said we would resort to anything rather than give up. 'Well,' replied the Yankee, 'I hope the South won't do anything of *that* kind, for of course in that event we would not spare or respect your women.'

MARCH 11TH.   A courier last night brought the news of the fall of Richmond—or at least its evacuation.[2] We have heard rumors to this effect for some time so we were in a measure prepared for it. It is so hard to believe. People talk about its being the best move, that now we will 'catch' Sherman, etc., etc. It seems nonsense to me. The fact remains that our capital, the great bone of contention for which the Yankees have struggled in vain for

2. The news was premature. It was not until March 26 that Lee notified President Davis the city of Richmond must be abandoned.

four years, around which so many bloody battles have been fought, has fallen at last. I feel as if the end had come, and utterly heartsick, and yet have become so accustomed to disaster that nothing overwhelms me, not even this. It only somewhat deepens the gloom. We *can not* be conquered—that is unthinkable—but these are bitter days, and we are passing through a dark cloud. Sherman marched through Georgia, Savannah fell—I thought he would be opposed here—the President promised to defend South Carolina, Sherman swept on unresisted, devastating, burning. He holds Charleston, has burned Columbia, left his whole track a smouldering desert. Now Richmond has fallen. Where is a ray of hope? Only to Gen. Lee and his poor little half-starved army can the people look—yet an army that has never suffered defeat, a contrast to the Western army.

MARCH 12TH. SUNDAY. It is a calm bright Spring day—warm, balmy and quiet. The Campus is quite green with the springing grass and the tall elms are budding. The birds are singing again and as we walked home from church this morning, we gathered blue hyacinths and yellow daffodils from among the blackened ruins. Spring no longer looks gay and bright as it used to in the fair town buried in trees and gardens, and even where the foliage is not destroyed the bursting green will make a sad contrast with the melancholy ruins. In church this morning all looked so familiar—the congregation full, Dr. Palmer in his place again, choir and organ—that sitting there it was hard to realize all was so changed. Coming out the ruins all around struck afresh with strangeness and unreality.

We have some one hundred and twenty of Wheeler's cavalry

here for a time, but they are going to leave. They were drawn up in the street this morning with forage at their backs.

Yesterday morning I spent with Aunt Jane, who is in bed thickly broken out with measles, more consequences of Walter's visit to us with them. In the afternoon I went to see Miss Jane and Miss Sophia Reynolds, and afterwards to Madame D'Ovilliers'. Nothing was talked of but that dreadful night. Poor little Madame, how she did jabber in her broken English. I will try to look up my friends, but many left before the surrender and most of the rest are burnt out and I do not know where to find them. Some (among them the Carrolls and Bauskets) went to Winnsboro' and met the Yankees there.

MARCH 14TH. Richmond has *not* fallen! Petersburg has been given up and Lee has drawn in his lines and sent 10,000 men to Johnston.[3] Aunt Jane has heard from Cousin John. She has been very uneasy about him, for when he came that fatal Friday to tell her goodbye, the Yankees were only two blocks behind him at the State House. He barely escaped by the fleetness of his horse but had to ride twenty-five miles through a deserted country to join his command and thinks he would have starved

3. Union forces did not occupy Petersburg until April 3, at four o'clock in the morning; Richmond officially surrendered four hours later. On March 16, Joseph E. Johnston was returned to the command of the Army of the South, though it had been anticipated for some time that he would do so; on March 19, Johnston and Sherman clashed in a bloody battle at Bentonville, N. C., where, it was said, the setting sun carried with it the last hopes of the Southern Confederacy. Lee's prospect of relief from this quarter had been crushed.

but for the large lunch Aunt Josie stuffed in his haversack as he left. Aunt Josie tried to look up some of our lost clothing. The authorities have taken everything stolen by the negroes or given them by the Yankees and exposed them in some building for identification by owners. Hearing that many articles were taken from Nitre Bureau negroes, Aunt Josie went forth with high hopes, but all she recovered was a portion of one of her dresses and the flounce of my green embroidered silk. She and Cousin Lula lost even more heavily than Mother and I in clothing, for we only sent off our best things, but they sent everything except two winter dresses apiece and hardly a change of underclothing, and not an article to begin Summer with. Our underclothing was all of homespun and our stockings homeknit, so we kept them. The silk dresses so carefully treasured during the war are entirely irreplaceable. Aunt Josie and Cousin Lula lost twenty-four between them. How are we to get clothes when even calico is from $25 to $30 a yard?

There is a report in town that Sherman has been killed, but that is far too good to be true. Another report is that Hampton fell in with part of his wagon train and captured the citizens who left Columbia with Sherman's army and recovered much silver stolen here. The Yankees said they had not anywhere met with such quantities of plate and valuables and plunder as they found in Columbia, that it seemed the richest place they had struck. They told the people of Cheraw (which was also burned) that they had treated Columbia worse than they should have done, but Sherman told them when they crossed the river that he would not restrain them, but gave them license to sack, pillage and burn the 'Capital of Secession' as they chose. [Several pages missing.]

MARCH 18TH. SATURDAY. We are looking for Father home now —we expected him yesterday or today. *At last* we have received some tidings from Charleston. Some people, unable any longer to endure the state of things, have found their way on foot to Columbia. The reign of terror they describe is unparalled even in this barbarous war. The city is garrisoned by negro troops who, unrestrained, perpetrate every barbarity, until at length their outrages reached such a pitch that their officers were obliged to some extent to interfere—thirty men were shot for violating women. In the surrounding country affairs are even worse than in the city—the slaves turned loose and wildest anarchy reigns. When some of Foster's[4] negro troops arrived in Georgetown the same excesses were begun there.

A Mr. Middleton, eighty years old, was ordered by ruffians to leave his house. He was alone, the family being here— he deprecated their cruelty, urging that he was old and had never taken any part in the war. They said they knew he was [a] darned old rebel, and ordered him to get out. He begged for a little time to move some effects—this being refused, he went to his room, put a few clothes in a pillowcase, and, taking a blanket from his bed, left the house. The negroes took his blanket from him. He watched his burning house till it was consumed and

4. General John A. Foster, Jr. On March 18, 1865, *Harper's Weekly* reported: ' . . . the first troops occupying the city [Charleston] were negroes under Colonel Bennett. On the night of the 21st [February] the Fifty-fifth Colored Massachusetts landed in the city and marched through the streets, singing the March of John Brown's Soul. If the war itself was a revolution of citizens against their Government, it has introduced also a revolution quite as profound in the relation hitherto existing between the negro and his master.'

then, taking the road to Columbia, walked the entire distance from Georgetown, reaching this place a day or two ago.

The people are fearing that a negro garrison may be sent here. If such fears should be realized, we must leave if we have to walk to Augusta. It is rumored that the Yankee gunboats are coming [up] the river to complete their work of destruction of Columbia by blowing up the State House. We hear so many wild and dreadful rumors. Mrs. Bird passed through yesterday on her way from Richmond to Augusta. She says the deepest despondency prevails there on account of the giving up of Charleston and Columbia and the expectation that Richmond will share the same fate. Charlotte stills holds out. We know almost nothing—the only reliable news from couriers and they come so rarely. It is wonderful the avidity with which every scrap of news or even rumor from the outer world is seized upon in this forlorn town. Mr. Pope has just got in. He says he only escaped by passing himself off as a preacher, and was several times told by the Yankees that they had caught tax-collector Pope. Most of them spoke exultingly of having burned Columbia—one only expressed regret because 'it was such a pretty town.' On his inquiring the cause of the conflagration, they at first repeated the story of the whiskey, but one fellow said frankly that he might as well tell the truth—that Sherman had ordered them to burn it, that they expected to burn it, and they *did* burn the hole of secession. Mr. Pope says that they had not, however, expected to take it, for Beauregard had telegraphed Hardee[5] to come to his aid, and that scoundrel paid no attention to the telegram.

5. General William J. Hardee

=⟨ *81* ⟩=

Mr. Pope says all the Yankees he talked with concurred in unqualified admiration for the pluck and dignity of the Columbia women. Through all the frightful night they did not see a tear or hear one complaint, and they did not think they could ever conquer the South if the men were animated by the same spirit as the women of South Carolina. Mr. Pope asked them if they thought to whip the South by marching through devastating the country, unopposed except by women and children. The Yankees replied that they did not expect to whip our armies, but meant to starve us out. 'And can you do that?' he asked; the Yankee said, 'Sometimes I doubt it, for everywhere we go we find such quantities of provisions. You Southerners have a rich country.' Telegraphic communication will be opened with Richmond in a few days and then I hope we will hear regularly from the armies in North Carolina and Virginia and also what has become of Thomas. We are also soon to have a tri-weekly paper edited by Gilmer Sims[6] and called 'The Phoenix'! I had saved almost a regular file of daily papers from 1862, but in the confusion of the fire they were emptied out of the trunk, scattered and destroyed.

Mother tried to persuade me to go with her to the depot, but I had no wish to see the dreadful sight. The ruins are filled with

6. William Gilmore Simms, novelist and poet. Largely through his auspices, a pamphlet entitled *Who Burnt Columbia?* was published in Charleston in 1875; included in its pages is the evidence on the sack and burning of Columbia as recorded by Simms, James G. Gibbes, and General Wade Hampton – extracts from the *Report of the Committee Appointed to Collect Testimony in Relation to the Destruction of Columbia, S. C. on the 17th of February, 1865* and from the testimony given in the case of J. J. Browne *v.* the United States.

the bones of the unfortunates who perished in the explosion, and their mangled remains are scattered around. The gas works, too, are destroyed beyond repair. When Father comes back, I think I will walk down to Granby and see the battlefield, though there is little to be seen, I suppose, beyond the breastworks and earth torn up and trees cut by cannon balls. The last news from Johnston was that he had retreated to Raleigh. This arch-retreater will probably retreat till perhaps he retreats to Gen. Lee, who may put a stop to his retrograde movement.

APRIL 1ST. Since my last entry on the 18th many events of importance have transpired. About ten days ago Father returned from Augusta bringing provisions, cloth, leather and *tallow* to make some candles—thus far we have had nothing but pine fire-light after dark. The provisions were flour, corn and bacon—a few hams, but chiefly the sides. I am so sick of bacon, it seems impossible for me to eat it. It seems as if I ought to when Father and the rest can eat it and think it good, but indeed my stomach turns against it and I usually make my dinner of hominy, corn bread and butter. The cloth is six bolts of factory cloth (un-bleached homespun) which Father, on account of being a 'Columbia sufferer,' got at the very low price of only three dollars a yard. It makes me groan in spirit to think of wearing this heavy stuff as underclothing all the hot summer. But, as Aunt Jane sagely observes, 'it is better than nothing.' Indeed, Cousin Ada and I agreed we would willingly wear sackcloth and even ashes if necessary, rather than give up to the Yankees. With all the ports closed, we will be obliged to give up every foreign luxury, which are even now by their high prices beyond the reach of all but speculators. As I sat with Aunt Jane (sick with the measles) we laughingly arranged it all and found we could live very well on home products. Our clothing is already mostly of homespun. Our stockings we already knit, and we make our own gloves. Our hats we could plait from palmetto or grass and trim them in Summer with natural flowers, in winter with holly berries and ivy. We have only a very few more things to learn in feminine dress.

Father brought us some nice fine yarn, so much pleasanter to use than the coarse stuff I got at the factory here, and I am now knitting with it some beautiful stockings. It would seem very strange now to put on a pair of new store stockings. And I am such an accomplished knitter that I do not look at my work and so can read and study while I knit. My hands are rarely without my knitting except when otherwise employed, and this has been a great resource during the long evenings with the light but dim firelight. Father brought us also some coarse blankets. The tallow Mother has moulded into candles. How we miss the gas! The evenings are so long and dismal by the light of a tallow candle. How unappreciated was this one luxury until we lost it. Mr. Stovall spent several days looking about the miserable wreck of Columbia.

We hear all sorts of vague rumors about Johnston defeating Sherman, but nothing definite enough to pin a hope to.

APRIL 13TH. Columbia was in quite a panic a few days ago. A Yankee raid was at Kingsville, and we feared it would shortly be here, but they turned off toward Camden. I heard a gentleman say he thought Columbia would be garrisoned this summer as a headquarters for sending out raids into the upper part of the State. They say there has been a fearful battle in Virginia—the most fearful battle of the war—that Lee has lost 20,000 men and fallen back, while Grant has lost 50,000.[7] We can ill afford to lose that number of men. All looks so dark and gloomy. I do not despair as many do, but I feel very sad and bitter when I think of the condition of our dear country.

The South *will* not give up—I can not think that—but I look forward to years of suffering and grief, years of desolation and bloodshed. They say Charlotte has fallen, Montgomery too and Selma—more than all, Richmond. All we have is those two armies, brave but outnumbered. If they are overthrown, then follows the wearing guerilla fighting and all the atrocities and evils that come in its train. I suppose the Yankees are holding a great jubilee in Charleston today. Not long ago they had a most absurd procession described in glowing colors and celebrating the Death of Slavery—Abolitionists delivered addresses on the superiority of the black race over white—Adam and Eve were black, so were Cain and Abel, but when the former slew his brother, his great fright turned him *white!* Also, 'As Christ died for the human race, so John Brown died for the negroes,' etc., etc.

Today they intended raising their wretched flag over noble

---

7. This reference is doubtless to the Battle of Five Forks, fought April 1. Against Lee's 10,600 cold and hungry Confederates the Union massed 10,000 cavalry and 43,000 infantry. The North cut off and captured over 3,200 prisoners while its own losses were less than 1,000. This battle sealed the fall of Petersburg, where, after ten months of vicious campaigning, Northern losses ran to 42,000 in killed, wounded, and captured, and Confederate casualties to more than 28,000.

old Sumter and there was to be a great to-do and fuss. Poor old Sumter—dear old fort! What a degradation! This day four long years ago. The joy—the excitement—how well I remember it. For weeks we had been in a fever of excitement. On the day the news came of the Fall of Sumter we were all sitting in the library at Uncle John's. The bell commenced to ring. At the first tap we knew the joyful tidings had come. Father and Uncle John made a dash for their hats—Jule and Johnny followed. We women ran trembling to the veranda—to the front gate, eagerly asking the news of passers-by. The whole town was in a joyful tumult. What could now rouse us from our dull apathy unless it were the certain news of an honorable peace. What changes— what a lifetime we have lived in the four years past!

I am studying German now and am working away at the grammar and translating Wilhelm Tell. I have long wanted to get a reading knowledge of this language and have eyed wistfully the sealed treasures of German literature in the library. So my pleasure can be conceived when Mrs. Leland offered to teach me in return for reading French with her. She and I have a conversation lesson of an hour and a half with Madame on Mondays and Thursdays at ten o'clock. On Wednesdays I read French with Mrs. Leland, and on Tuesdays and Fridays we have a German class, Mrs. Leland giving us generally two hours as she has much leisure. Indeed, I would be sorry to leave Columbia and the libraries now with these nice plans on hand.

APRIL 14TH. I am so thankful that winter has gone finally and entirely. Cold weather means real suffering in many ways to us and bright spring is doubly welcome. She did not come coquet-

'Hurrah! Old Abe Lincoln has been Assassinated!'

ting as last year, but, as it were, rushed into our arms. In the space of two weeks the trees burst into leaf, so rapidly that one could almost see them unfolding. By the first of April they were in full foliage. Those parts of town, like the Campus, that were untouched by the fire are now lovely with the delicate green of spring. Among the ruins one sees long avenues of burnt and blackened trees—now and then in mocking contrast one will stretch its leafy branches over a crumbling wall, and sometimes half or part of a tree has struggled into leaf and the rest stands gaunt and bare.

Christ Church was one of the last buildings burned. It makes a beautiful ruin, especially now when through the tall gothic windows and above the pointed walls one sees the waving foliage of Blanding Street. Here in the Campus nothing mars the springtime beauty—it is lovely. I am sitting in the front door and the afternoon is deepening into twilight. The grass is fresh and green under the majestic elms whose wide-spreading, sweeping branches, so black and fine, show out in relief against the tender green of the young leafage. The oaks, too, are all out, and so thick is the mass of verdure that from my bedroom windows I cannot see across to the library building with its white columns. Just before me on the green lawn beneath a great elm is pitched a tent or large fly under which are lying half-a-dozen soldiers. At a little distance two fires are burning and around them are grouped others busily engaged in preparing their evening meal. These men are just from Camden—'to them,' as Goethe says, 'the old story of the year is being repeated again.' We are come again, thank God, to its most charming chapter. The violets and May flowers are its superscription and vignettes. It always makes a pleasant impression on us when we open at these pages of the 'book of life.'

We, Father, Cousin Ada and I, walked into the woods yesterday afternoon. We found the ground fairly carpeted with violets, phlox and other spring flowers. We gathered large bunches of them and sat a long time on the mosses of the Rocky Branch just where the water makes a mimic cataract over large rocks. I am always so happy when I get into the country.

APRIL 16TH. SATURDAY. Went out this morning to have our feet measured for shoes. Oliver's shop is a genuine phoenix risen from its ashes. He has built a frame building of two rooms around his old chimney. Coming back we passed through the State House yard, picking our way over piles of rubbish. On every side a wilderness of granite and marble. Piles on piles of white and Tennessee marble blocks, cracked, broken and smoke-begrimed. Many blocks are crumbling to pieces—even the granite slabs are cracked and scaling from the heat of the burning workshops and sheds. Hundreds of sculptured capitals lie broken and defaced. In the midst rises the half-finished capital seeming to look mournfully down on the destruction that surrounds it. In a remote part of the grounds behind some granite blocks lie scattered the Chimes of St. Michael's—one quite destroyed, all cracked by the heat. Those historic bells, ten in number, [are] considered the finest chime in the country. They were presented from the mother country while South Carolina was a colony. When Charleston was taken by the British, the bells were sent to England. After the Revolution some say they were returned, others that they were brought back—anyway, they came back to Charles-

=〈 *88* 〉=

ton and for eighty years played from St. Michael's tower. Two years ago, when bells were given to be moulded into cannon, they were sent here, either for that purpose or for safe keeping while Charleston was under fire. They were placed in a building on the State House grounds, and here they lie now. (Footnote added later—After the war these bells were sent to England and re-cast in the same foundry where they were originally made, and they now hang in St. Michael's steeple.)

News came today that Camden *was* taken by the raiders, so there is some chance of getting our rice after all (rice stored there belonging to the Nitre Bureau).

Gen. Lovell[8] has been appointed to the command of the Department of South Carolina. I hope he will infuse some spirit into our people and defend us from the Yankees.

[Several pages are here missing. The journal is resumed about April 20th, after the news of Lee's surrender had been received, and after the fall of Richmond.]

* * * (armistice or truce (?) between) Generals Johnston and Sherman not to be broken without forty-eight hours notice. Couriers have been despatched to stop Stoneman's[9] raid at Camden. What it is I do not know, but it can bode no good to us. This the Grand Army of Virginia which has heretofore never known defeat, but has stood like some great rock against which the huge waves of our enemies have dashed themselves in vain, is now

8. Mansfield Lovell. As early as 1862 Mrs. Chesnut grouped him with those 'men born Yankees' who were 'an unlucky selection as commanders of the Confederacy,' since 'they believe in the North in a way no true Southerner ever will, and they see no shame in surrendering to the Yankees.' *Chesnut*, 217.

9. General George Stoneman

melted away. All that is left is Johnston's small army, cooped up between Grant's hordes on the one hand and Sherman's on the other. Wiser heads than mine say it must surrender, and then the waves will roll over us.

The South lies prostrate—their foot is on us—there is no help. During this short time we breathe, but—oh, who could have believed who has watched this four years' struggle that it could have ended like this! They say *right* always triumphs, but what cause could have been more just than ours? Have we suffered all—have our brave men fought so desperately and died so nobly for *this*? For four years there has been throughout this broad land little else than the anguish of anxiety—the misery of sorrow over dear ones sacrificed—for *nothing*! Is all this blood spilled in vain—will it not cry from the ground on the day we yield to these Yankees! *We* give up to the *Yankees*! How *can* it be? How can they talk about it? Why does not the President call out the women if there are [not] enough men? We would go and *fight*, too—we would better all die together. Let us suffer still more, give up yet more—anything, anything that will help the cause, anything that will give us freedom and not force us to live with such people—to be ruled by such horrible and contemptible creatures—to submit to them when we hate them so bitterly.

It is cruel—it is *unjust*. I used to dream about peace, to pray for it, but this is worse than war. What is such peace to us? What horrible fate has been pursuing us the last six months? Not much farther back than that we had every reason to hope for success. What is the cause of this sudden crushing collapse? I *cannot* understand it. I never loved my country as I do now. I feel I could sacrifice *everything* to it, and when I think of the future—

oh God! It is too horrible. What I most fear is a conciliatory policy from the North, that they will offer to let us come back as before. Oh, no, no! I would rather we were held as a conquered province, rather sullenly submit and bide our time. Let them oppress and tyrannize, but let us take no favors of them. Let them send us away out of the country—anywhere away from them and their hateful presence.

We are all very wretched. Poor Father! He had Carrie in his arms just now, but her innocent joy and laughter so grated upon him that he had to send her away. It seems dreadful to see anyone smile. It seems impossible to utterly despair. If we did we would be even more miserable than we are. We feel instinctively that something must happen to avert our doom. It is so terrible as to be unthinkable. We have been so confident of final success that we *cannot* believe we are conquered. What misfortune will I have to chronicle tomorrow. I am too sick at heart to write any more.

FRIDAY. Hurrah! Old Abe Lincoln has been assassinated![1] It may be abstractly wrong to be so jubilant, but I just can't help it. After all the heaviness and gloom of yesterday this blow to our enemies comes like a gleam of light. We have suffered till we feel savage. There seems no reason to exult, for this will make no change in our position—will only infuriate them against us. Never mind, our hated enemy has met the just reward of his life. The whole story may be a Yankee lie. The despatch purports to be from Stanton[2] to Sherman. It says Lincoln was murdered

1. Lincoln, shot by John Wilkes Booth, died the following morning at 7:22 o'clock.

2. Edward M. Stanton, Secretary of War

in his private box at the theatre on the night of the 14th (Good Friday—at the *theatre*). The assassin brandished a dagger and shouting, 'Sic semper tyrannis—Virginia is avenged,' shot the President through the head. He fell senseless and expired next day a little after ten. The assassin made his escape in the crowd. No doubt it was regularly planned and he was surrounded by Southern sympathizers.[3] 'Sic semper tyrannis.' Could there have been a fitter death for such a man? At the same hour nearby Seward's[4] house was entered—he was badly wounded as also his son. Why could not the assassin have done his work more thoroughly? That *vile* Seward—he it is to whom we owe this war—it is a shame he should escape.

I was at Mrs. Leland's saying my German when Mrs. Snowden brought in the news. We were all so excited and talked so much that Wilhelm Tell was quite forgotten. Our spirits had been so low that the least good news elevated them wonderfully and this was so utterly unlooked-for, took us so completely by surprise. I actually *flew* home and for the first time in oh, so long, I was trembling and my heart beating with excitement. I stopped in at Aunt Josie's to talk it over.

As soon as I reached the head of the stairs, they all cried,

3. Emma expresses an opinion which the Union government tried vainly to prove at the subsequent trial of Booth's conspirators. It was claimed that many persons high in the Confederate government had been involved in this plot not only to kill the President but also General Grant and principal Cabinet officers.

4. William H. Seward, Secretary of State, who was sick at home. Lewis Payne, one of Booth's accomplices, subsequently executed for the crime, forced his way past Seward's son and stabbed the Secretary three times. Payne fled from the house shouting, "I am mad! I am mad!"

'Hurrah! Old Abe Lincoln has been Assassinated!'

'What do you think of the news?' 'Isn't it splendid,' etc. We were all in a tremor of excitement. At home it was the same. If it is *only* true! The first feeling I had when the news was announced was simply gratified revenge. The man we hated has met his proper fate. I thought with exultation of the howl it had by that time sent through the North, and how it would cast a damper on their rejoicings over the fall of our noble Lee. The next thought was how it would infuriate them against us—and that was pleasant, too. After talking it over, the hope presented itself that it might produce a confusion that would be favorable, but there is scarcely any likelihood of that—he is hardly important enough for that. Andy Johnson[5] will succeed him—the rail-splitter will be succeeded by the drunken ass. Such are the successors of Washington and Jefferson, such are to rule the South. 'Sic semper tyrannis'—it has run in my head all day.

> "Tremblez tyrans! et vous perfides
> L'opprobres de toutes les parties—
> Tremblez! vos projets parricides
> Font *enfin* recevoir leur prix!"

What exciting, what eventful times we are living in!

---

5. Andrew Johnson, a Democrat, a Southerner and a former slave-owner. The touchy pride of a self-made man was his gravest weakness; a man who had come from extremely humble beginnings, without the least formal education, this one-time tailor's apprentice became President surrounded by enemies. Republicans were determined to hold their power, Southerners never forgave Johnson for remaining loyal to the Union. An effort to impeach him succeeded but he was acquitted.

6

'What Tyranny'

APRIL 23RD. SUNDAY.   Dr. Palmer this morning preached a fine and encouraging sermon. He says we must not despair yet, but even if we should be overthrown—not conquered—the next generation would see the South *free* and independent.

There is another rumor in town to the effect that the French fleet has defeated the Yankee fleet and taken New Orleans. It is only a rumor, and alas, I dare not believe it. The air is so full of rumors that one does not know what to believe—they only keep us in a feverish state of uncertainty.

The more I think of Lee's surrender the harder it is to bear. That army—that General—we idolized Stonewall Jackson, worshipped Lee. It is perhaps well that [the] President has so many enemies, for if all loved [him] as the others, something would happen to him too.

How well I remember the death of Stonewall Jackson! I can never forget my feelings when I heard of it. We had heard he was very low, but I did not dream *he* could *die*. I was lying on the lounge alone in the library when Father came in looking very sad. 'Emma,' he said gravely, 'Stonewall Jackson is dead.' How I loved him! He was my hero. I then admired Lee as grand, magnificent, but Jackson came nearer my heart. There was mourning deep and true throughout the land when that news came.

Since then Lee has had the hero-worship, *all*—both his and Jackson's—though the dead hero will always be shrined in every Southern heart. But I am allowing old reminiscences to fill my mind and page. Not so old either—only two years—but events have crowded so thickly that it seems a long, long time ago. Our beloved Lee! Now that the first crushing grief for the country is passed in some measure away, how deeply I feel for *him*—how he must suffer—not only the humiliation, but to hold his hands in this hour of his country's greatest need. What must it have meant to him to yield that sword! And what are we to do without him!

I cannot feel hopeless. Today I do not feel as disheartened as I did last Thursday when the news came—the terrible news. We still have an army in the West, and dark as everything is, we *must* hope. The conviction that the South can *not* be conquered, that it can *never* be reunited with the North, is so deeply rooted in my heart. Since the war began, that conviction has never been shaken once till last Thursday. Then I was so overwhelmed by the thought of Lee's surrender that there seemed no ground under my feet. Even now there can be no hope but in foreign aid. But something *must* turn up—help *must* come—'The darkest hour's before the dawn.' If there should be no dawn!

MAY 2ND. My last entry was not quite ten days ago. It seems like months, we have suffered so much since. Then we were buoyed up by the hope of foreign intervention and by Lincoln's assassination. It was confidently affirmed that our President had said in a speech at Charleston that the French had promised intervention and our darkest days were passed. I do not know that the President ever made a speech there or said such words, but we believed it. A thousand rumors filled the air. Now the French fleet was at New Orleans—now at Beaufort, now at Georgetown, and finally it was confidently stated that this ubiquitous fleet had defeated the Yankees at Hampton Roads. I will *never* believe another French rumor nor any other rumor that means hope to this unhappy land. Nothing good can come— fate has heaped upon us miseries and misfortunes that could not even have been dreamed of by us. The only question now is not 'What hope?', but 'What new bitterness?'

On the Sunday night of my last entry (the 23rd) Cousin Willie came from Europe by way of the North. Succeeding at last in reaching his native land, eager to join her struggle for freedom, in what condition does he find her! Monday morning I was returning from my French when Sallie called me into the library to see him. I found a boy of nineteen—rather short, with a pleasant and real 'LeConte' face. I was prepared to like him because of the patriotism that sent him to a failing cause. We did not rush very fast into an acquaintanceship, both being rather shy, but I like him better every day and if he stays long enough, I think we will be good friends. He spent a week at Aunt Josie's and then came over here where he still is.

MAY 17TH. WEDNESDAY.   I have not touched my journal for two weeks. When I tried to chronicle the painful events transpiring I found I could not. It would not only take too much time, but perhaps it is best not to put all I felt and suffered on paper. One of these days I may think those feelings were wicked. The fall of the Confederacy so crushed us that it seemed to me I did not care what became of me. It is impossible not to feel rebellious and bitter. It is impossible not to feel that it is unjust and cruel. And so I had better not write about it all—only of personal and family matters, if I can keep back the expression of what fills my heart and thoughts.   PLANS to stop HATRED !!

The troops are coming home. One meets long-absent, familiar faces on the streets, and congregations once almost strictly feminine are now mingled with returned soldiers. Our boys—Cousin Johnny and Julian—have come home, too. It was pleasant to see them again, but the meeting was more sad than glad. We would have waited many years if only we could have received them back triumphant. For four years we have looked forward to this day—the day when the troops would march home. We expected to meet them exulting and victorious. That was to be a day of wildest joy, when the tidings of peace should reach us, and the thought of that time used to lighten our hearts and nerve us to bear every trial and privation. Then we determined, after our independence was acknowledged and the time came for Gen. Lee to disband his army, to go on to Richmond to see the glorious sight, to see the hero take leave of his brave victorious men. The army is disbanded now—oh! Merciful God!—the hot tears rush into my eyes and I cannot write.

Cousin Johnny came first and about a week later Julian. We were not expecting Jule so soon. It was lovely moonlight night and we—both households—had agreed to walk together over the town and view the ruins by the full moon. We had not gone more than two or three blocks when we met a rough soldier with knapsack and blanket roll on his back. The meeting may be better imagined than described. After much embracing, kissing, chattering and some tears Julian, who was too tired to go with us, went on home to his mother accompanied by Uncle John and Johnny, while the rest of us pursued our walk. Cousin Johnny came home quite broken down, but Jule seems very well except that his feet are blistered so that he can hardly walk. He is of course paroled.

I must say something of that walk among the ruins. It was very beautiful and melancholy. I wish I had a picture of that scene. Everything was still as death. The only sounds that broke the silence were our footsteps among the rubbish, and sometimes the low voices of our party. There was little talking—the weird scene seemed to cast a spell upon us. As far as the eye could reach only spectre-like chimneys and the shattered walls, all flooded over by the rich moonlight which gave them a mysterious but mellow softness, and quite took from them the ghastly air which they wear in the sunlight. They only lacked moss and lichens and tangled vines to make us believe we stood in some ruined city of antiquity.

We walked down Sumter Street and turned into Blanding.

This was still more beautiful, for the handsome residences made most picturesque ruins. Clarkson's house with its white columns gleaming in the moonlight looked like an old Greek ruin. And for some reason—perhaps the large lots and greater distances between the houses—the trees and shrubbery on this street have been almost unscorched and make masses of foliage about the crumbling walls. At last we reached Christ Church—it was a very pretty little church, and makes a lovely ruin. It was charming in this mystic light. As we stood before it, the moon shone full upon us through the big arched window. We stood gazing on it in silence for many minutes. Had the walls only been mantled with ivy and a few sharp outlines softened by time and clinging lichens it would have been perfect. The walls are entire almost and firm, and we went up the stone steps and viewed the interior from the entrance. Retracing our steps, we walked across to Main Street and walked down that former thoroughfare trying to imagine it as it once was. We took a peep up the tall tower of the market, and sat on the fallen bell. As we walked down the middle of the street, the great State House shone white before us, looking itself like a grand ruin. We would have liked to have taken a comprehensive view from the top of its walls, but the Yankees had burned out the temporary floors and stairsteps, leaving only the walls like a shell.

We had started out at eight and it was ten when we got to Aunt Josie's and found Julian waiting for us, quite tired and anxious to get to bed. We enjoy having the boys back and in spite of all depressing influences, have pleasant days. Young people cannot be depressed and gloomy *all* the time. There are eight of us altogether, between the ages of fourteen and twenty-four, and it is nice to have the boys home even if they are returned like this.

We walk in the woods afternoons—generally down to Gregg's spring, where we sit and talk and laugh and tease each other till almost dark. The last two afternoons we walked to the river. Cousin John Harden and Willie LeConte leave us next Monday. The former goes to the plantation (in Liberty County, Ga.), and the latter to his uncle, Gen. W. L. Smith in Athens, and we resolve that this last week of their stay shall be a merry one. They promised to meet here every evening for a dance. Accordingly, Monday evening the whole contingent from the other house came over and we had a jolly time. Tuesday evening was, if anything, even livelier. Our spirits seemed to rise at the sound of the piano and we went into it with a vim, especially Cousin John. How long it had been since any of us had danced! It did seem heartless, perhaps, but we could not help enjoying it, and it seemed such a relief to throw off the trouble and gloom for a little while—and it was only among ourselves. I will be sorry when two of the cousins leave us—we will miss them so much, and it will be very dull without them. Jule is quieter and Johnny is much younger. And the girls will predominate—now we are evenly divided.

THURSDAY.   We were visited yesterday by a squad of Yankees under Lieut. Brett, the first that have been in Columbia since the 20th of February. They bring a message to Governor Magrath. Magrath, with the fate of the governor of North Carolina before his eyes, had 'skedaddled.'[1] Thereupon the blue devils fastened their horses and sat themselves down in the Campus to await his return. The negroes throng around them and they affiliate pleasantly with their colored brethren—even affectionately. They lie beside them on the grass and walk the streets with the negro girls, calling them 'young ladies'—and why not? Doubtless they recognize in them not only their equals, but their superiors. *Perhaps* negroes *may* come in contact with them without being degraded, but I doubt it, for the negro is an imitative race. He has been elevated to some extent but will quickly retrograde in associating with such white people as these. Dear me! How the sight of that blue uniform makes my blood boil! They are camping just in front of the house so that I cannot go to the front door or windows without seeing their hateful forms, and [the] sight fills me with such horrid feelings that I keep in the back parlor and dining room and close the blinds when I go to my bedroom. Yesterday I went into the library for a book. The sash-door was

1. In North Carolina a Raleigh newspaper editor, William W. Holden, whom *Harper's Weekly* described as 'a gentleman who has not been sincerely a rebel, and who heartily rejoices at the overthrow of the rebel despotism,' had been named provisional governor. Holden accepted emancipation; he would educate the Negro, recognize his marriage relations, let him hold property, but 'beyond that I leave him to the future action of the States themselves. . . . The whole vast continent is destined to fall under the control of the Anglo-Saxon race—the governing and self-governing race. I look to the wisdom of the people in the Convention to decide the relations of the two races.' Holden went too far for the South, and not far enough for the North; Holden, declared the editors of *Harper's Weekly* for June 3, 1865, was a perfect example of one 'whose heart is right, but whose head is wrong'; for one class of citizens to decide whether another class should vote or even be allowed to remain in the State 'certainly does not seem to us the road that leads to peace.'

open and I saw them sitting and lying about on the grass. Before I knew it my hands were clinched, and such a feeling came into my heart as startled me and I fled upstairs away from the sight of them. These men seem to be the meanest type of the mean nation. Their presence has put an end to our pleasant evening reunions, to our walks, in fact to everything.

AFTERNOON.   This morning we received the last crowning piece of bad news. I did not think it possible anything worse could happen. We heard of the capture of President Davis![2] This is dreadful, not only because we love him, but because it gives the final blow to our cause. If he could have reached the West he might have rallied the army out there and continued the resistance. But now where can we look for a head? I was studying my German when Father came in and told me. I laid my head on the table without a word. I did not cry—the days of weeping are past—but, ah! the heartache—the only thing left to hear now is the surrender of the army in the West and that must come pretty soon. I think I have given up hope at last, at least for the present. We will be conquered. Only in the future can we still hope, either for a foreign war in which we can join the enemies of the United States, or else that after years of recuperation we may be strong enough and, wiser by experience, renew the struggle and throw off the hateful yoke. The only other chance is that by their oppression and insolence they may drive the people to guerilla warfare and be wearied out at last.

2. President Davis was captured at Irwinsville, Georgia, on the morning of May 10.

MAY 23RD. TUESDAY.   Gov. Magrath arrived Saturday and on Sunday morning the Yankees left carrying some three hundred negroes with them. The message to Magrath was about his proclamation concerning seizing Confederate property. It seems the Yankees took this in high dudgeon, regarding it as theirs. We took our last walk together Monday afternoon and our last little dance on Monday evening, for they did not leave till this morning, but I do not think our hearts were much in it for we could not feel the approaching separation. They started at 5 a.m. to walk to Augusta, and I was up to see them off. I miss Cousin Willie very much—he has been in the house so long that he seemed quite one of us, and I have grown very much attached to him.

An order was sent to Gen. Lovell for distribution—the sense was about as follows: 'Whereas one Magrath styling himself Governor of South Carolina has issued a proclamation ordering the seizure of all Confederate property within the limits of the state,

'And whereas one Joseph Brown[3] styling himself Governor of Georgia has published an order convening the legislature, and whereas one Alison[4] styling himself Governor of Florida has taken steps for the election of a Governor for that state,

'Be it known to all citizens of the aforesaid states that such orders and proclamations are null and void, and that the status of said states will hereafter be decided by the proper authorities and

3. Joseph E. Brown, never popular because of his high-handed ways, had acted as though he were above Davis and the Confederacy in administering the affairs of Georgia.

4. A. K. Alison

at the proper time.' And 'that the slaves are to be considered free, but are advised to work as before for their former masters as the United States will not tolerate idleness.' It is signed, Gilmore.[5]

Is this not insolent? Gen. Lovell put it in his pocket and refused to give it circulation.

MAY 28TH. SUNDAY.   I do not attempt to write regularly now. I have lost all interest in keeping this fragmentary record—in fact everything. I must try to get interested again in studying and reading, try to get my thoughts away from the country. It is very hard to do this. Such things have for so long been neglected, I have lost interest and I think Father has, too. During this long vacation he has asked me once or twice why I do not commence again, but I can see he is indifferent. We are all indifferent and nothing short of excitement can rouse interest in anything. Yet I feel I must study—an education now is more important to me than ever. The only work I can look forward to is teaching and ought to be studying all I can. I have not been absolutely idle, for I have continued to teach Sallie regularly.

Last Thursday the garrison arrived. It consists of one regiment under Col. Horton[Haughton?]—another is expected shortly. Col. Horton and his men [are] Westerners. He seems to be a gentleman and his men are under strict discipline. They molest no one and are polite. I am glad to say they are introducing some order in town—it is sadly needed—and setting the negroes to work. These men, so far from fraternizing with the negroes, seem to hold them in profound disgust. The people avoid the

5. General Quincy A. Gilmore

soldiers and have nothing to do with them except on business, neither do they offer them any form of insult. The regiment is encamped back of the Campus, but one company comes inside every morning as a guard to Col. Horton who has his headquarters in the Campus a few doors from our house. So we still have them before our eyes. The soldiers behave so well—indeed, there are guards on every street—that ladies are beginning to walk freely out when it is absolutely necessary. I only go out to my lessons and occasionally to Aunt Josie's.

The first time I went out to my German it was almost amusing. There was a sentinel at the Campus gate and, as I had the same invincible horror of passing him that one would have to a very loathsome reptile, I thought I would go through Aunt Josie's yard into the street. But when I got beyond the gate I saw there were two standing between me and the side gate. I hesitated and walked very slowly, hoping they would move off. I started to turn back but Mother was in the door watching and laughing at me. So I doubled my veil, raised my parasol and passed swiftly and boldly between them, for they were several yards apart. I have grown a little more used to them after several days, but I still feel a shudder when I pass within twenty yards of one. Consequently, I always avoid the guard at the gate by going across through Aunt Josie's. This morning, though, I went through with the rest of the family going to Church and was obliged to pass so near one who was sitting on the ground that I had to hold my skirts back for fear my dress might accidentally touch him. Listen! They are beating Tattoo now—that disgusting Yankee Doodle. And they have dress parade every morning just opposite the Campus.

MAY 29TH. MONDAY. I went to French this morning. These conversation lessons are very pleasant but I do not know how long I can be allowed to enjoy them. True, Madame's prices are very low, but when it is all we can do to live, everything is high I pay her in provisions at the rate of ten cents an hour, but our supply is diminishing very fast and we cannot tell where more is to come from.

Poor Father is looking very badly, too, and is very much troubled. He can get no employment and not one cent of money in the house. He hopes when the railroad is completed there may be some trade and business here and he can then get work, but that will be quite a while yet. In the meantime a flatboat belonging to the Nitre Bureau has been secured to Father by Uncle John in payment of salary due. This through the kindness of Horton, to whom Father went to ask that the boat be not confiscated but that he allow it to be disposed of in this way. James Gibbes wants Father to bring up corn for the city with this boat, and the tithe that he gets therefrom will keep our two families for awhile. It is pretty bad but I do not think we will starve. We have been very low several times but something always turns up at the last moment.

They are administering the oath here now and almost everyone is obliged to take it, for unless they do, they are not allowed to engage in any occupation, nor to travel beyond the limits of the town, nor will they be protected against violence or injustice of any kind. Aunt Josie says, and I suppose they reason in the same way, that she would take it as a mere form forced upon her and therefore not binding on her conscience, and that she would break it as readily as she would take it. But I cannot feel that way and I do not see how I could do it unless really starving. Father, too, feels that it would be a most painful necessity that would compel him to such a humiliation. Well, I do not suppose it will be required of women, and I hope Father will be spared the swallowing this bitter pill on account of his being a paroled officer. I saw a copy of the oath yesterday. It requires you to repudiate all allegiance to the so-called Confederate States and only permits loyalty to your own state so long as that state is not opposed to the United States, thus putting allegiance to the U. S. Government *above* that to the *state*. You then have to swear allegiance to the U. S. Government, binding yourself in the most solemn way to uphold it under all circumstances, and all this is sworn 'without mental reservation or secret evasion, so help me God.' Who could take such an oath as that? It is a tyrannical measure to force it upon the Southern people. Ministers are not allowed to preach without taking it and I hear Mr. Shand has had to submit to it. If we could *only* leave the country—will we ever have the means to do so? How could we ever raise the money? We dream of this and make plans to emigrate—but the means are lacking now. We will have to wait. But I would rather work hard for my daily bread than live in luxury under Yankee rule.

These Yankee officers who behave like gentlemen—if Yankees *can* be gentlemen—take it rather hard that they are treated so coldly and allowed no social intercourse with the citizens. Horton especially seems to feel it that he is cut off so absolutely from the society of ladies. Great Heavens! What do they expect? They invade our country, murder our people, desolate our homes, conquer us, subject us to every indignity and humiliation—and then we must offer our hands with pleasant smiles and invite them to our houses, entertain them perhaps with 'Southern hospitality'—all because sometimes they act with common decency and humanity! Are they crazy? What do they think we are made of? * * * [*A hiatus of about a month comes here.*]

JUNE 27TH. A whole day before me to read without interruption—what a luxury! Mrs. Leland told me when I called for her at Madame's yesterday that she would not be able to meet her German class this afternoon, so I have not those twelve or fourteen pages of German to translate and can put the time into reading besides having the whole afternoon to myself. I have made up my room and finished with Sallie's lessons and with my books before me cannot linger long over this, I think. In history I am still on old Gibbon but getting through him as fast as I can, as I am anxious to begin Michelet's 'Histoire de France.' I happened to be reading on Mohamet and his doctrine so have dipped into the Koran which I will read through *if I can.* I am also reading a volume of Carlyle's Essays—I like Carlyle very much. I am getting back to my books all right as far as reading is concerned—I begin again to find them a blessed resource—to be able to lose myself in their world and forget the world of trouble around me. But when it comes to study, I do not find it so easy. In the long interval I seem to have lost the power of close application and systematic regularity and with no outward stimulus it is pretty hard. But I have made a start. Till Father can again give me instruction, I have decided to review arithmetic and algebra with a view to possibly being able to get an assistant teacher's place. The higher mathematics I do not think it will be necessary to freshen up on as I would not be expected to teach them at my age. It may not be necessary for me to get work and I may not be able to get it, but the review can do me no harm in any event. I wish I could get some employment *now*, anything, no matter what. If only I could make a little money—ever so little—just to help Father a little bit. We subsist now on the little Father makes from his flatboat. He brings up corn for the town and gets a tenth which is divided between him and Uncle John and Capt. Green. We hope for a little improvement in business when the railroad is finished.

Gen. Hartwell[6] is in town again, the vile, miserable tyrant. He came up here not long ago. I suppose he thought things were going on too smoothly and comfortably under Haughton[7] and he was needed to stir up a fuss and make the people realize their position. He is a friend of Prof. Pierce and immediately called on Uncle John to deliver messages from him and make enquiries. The first thing he did was to take possession of Mrs. Bausket's house, which she had left for a short visit to her plantation, and there he established himself and proceeded to hold his orgies. The next thing he did was to go to Church. After the service he wrote a note to Mr. Shand saying he had observed the omission of the prayer for the President of the United States, and that Mr. Shand would be pleased to use it hereafter or he would be under the unpleasant necessity of closing his Church. (Closing a Church at present means giving it to the negroes.) A few days after he left for a week or two. Mr. Shand went to Col.

6. Alfred S. Hartwell

7. Colonel Nathaniel Haughton

Haughton about it. The Colonel told him he was very sorry, but since the thing was brought before him officially, he was compelled to carry out his orders. 'I have,' he said, 'abstained from going to Church ever since I have been here because I understood the prayer was not used and I did not wish to interfere with your religious worship.' The next Sunday Col. Haughton went to Church and the prayer was used. At the first words the congregation rose from their knees. Mr. Shand hurried through it as if the words choked him, and at the end not one *amen* was heard throughout the Church, not even from the minister who was assisting at the altar. Cousin Lula says she felt her blood begin to boil as she heard that villainous wretch prayed for! Did ever anyone hear of such tyranny as forcing a *prayer* on people? What has the government to do with the Church? There is no union of church and state in this country.

Gen. Hartwell has called on Uncle John again this time. He mentioned that he wished to provision the town and relieve the suffering here, that he could bring supplies to Fort Mott by steamer, but would need boats to transport them to Columbia. Father accordingly went to see him to try to make arrangements for hiring his boat to him. He is very willing to take it. As Father went out, in order to apologize as it were for his deep anxiety, he remarked that this seemed a piddling sort of business to be so much interested in and one in which he had never been accustomed to engage. 'But,' he added, 'the fact is, General, the subsistence of our two families depends on it.' The remark seemed to strike Hartwell, and I suppose he thought on it. At all events he called on Uncle John in the afternoon and offered to lend either of them as much money as they wished. He said he knew it was a delicate offer to make and he was fully aware of the bitterness of feeling that existed at present, but if they hesitated to accept it from him, at least they might draw on Pierce and he would honor the draft. Of course his offer was declined. As long as we can keep body and soul together, Father would not borrow from anybody, but to be under obligations to a *Yankee!*

We have corn, a little flour and a few vegetables from the garden. For several weeks we have not had any meat until the past few days when Mother has bought a little bacon with the proceeds of her buttermilk, but I cannot eat bacon—especially this hot weather. Yesterday we had a little piece of beef—a luxury indeed—the first we have tasted since Sherman passed through. It is the last of June, but we have had no fruit except blackberries and wild plums, although I hear it is a plentiful fruit season. Madame gave me three large figs yesterday. The Yankees are issuing rations but they are only drawn by people in actual need or who have no self-respect.

Jane left us yesterday, having only informed Mother the day before of her intended departure. She was a great nuisance, but her leaving so unexpectedly caused us some inconvenience as we had to take care of Carrie. If she can get a nurse for her food, she will do so and we will do the house work between us. I wish she could clear out the whole of them—we have them to feed and get very little out of them in return.

WEDNESDAY. We have the unprecedented rains, but yesterday the sun came out to the joy of everyone. I walked in the afternoon to the Park with Lawrence Reynolds. After tea Mr. and

Miss B. Called. Mr. B. is very pleasant, but not, I judge, over-burdened with brains. Sallie and some of her friends had two dances here last week, on Wednesday and Friday evenings. Both evenings were rainy and I had to join in to help them out. Cousins Lula and Ada came over Friday evening to look on. Lawrence came and played for them on his violin, which, how-ever, was minus one string— a deficiency that could not be sup-plied—and some of the music in consequence [was] rather curi-ous. Mr. Hayne dropped in later and we made a group of older folks in the back parlor while the juveniles danced in the front.

When Hartwell came back the other day he brought a Gen. Hatch[8] with him. So they are both at Mrs. Bausket's, who as soon as she heard of the state of affairs hurried back to Columbia and, calling on Gen. Hatch, demanded her house. He treated her insolently. She spoke her mind rather freely, and he threat-ened to arrest her. He got spiteful and declared she shall not have her house at all. The two tyrants leave Columbia next week, I think. It is almost impossible to tell of all they do, and besides, we are grown so used to it now.

JULY 5TH. Yesterday the negroes had their grand celebration which has been talked of for the past two months. The white people shut themselves within doors and the darkies had the day to themselves—they and the Yankees. It was a fearfully warm day and some four or five thousand negroes assembled in Colum-bia. To prevent any disturbance, Col. [Haughton] ordered two regiments who were on their way up the country to stop on the

8. John P. Hatch

other side of the river until after the Fourth. Most of the gentle-men of the town were invited, but of course not one *real* gentleman was present. Father's invitation was given him last Thursday, and when I came in from Madame's, Mother handed it to me, saying, 'Let us see what she will say.' She and Father were greatly amused at the expression of surprise, and then of supreme scorn that overspread my face as I read. I was highly indignant and regarded it as a piece of insolent impudence, but Father said he thought it was meant kindly.

I had dreaded the cannonading, for it was said eighty blank cartridges were sent up for the occasion and the cannon was to be planted at the Campus gate. I expected to be aroused by day-light but was agreeably disappointed, for not one was fired the whole day. I could have listened to the roar of cannon at our very doors all day and thought it music were it celebrating *our* independence and—but well, well—what is the use of talking about it. The immense procession was marshalled down until it reached the College Hall, where they listened to an address from Col. Haughton, one from an abolition lawyer from Philadelphia, and two or three negroes. The poor old Hall where the students used to spout at their Commencements, and where at the begin-ning of the war when they organized as the 'College Cadets' was presented to them, with much speechifying, the flag given by the ladies—oh, who then [could] have imagined its being put to *this* use! Such horrid degradation!

On this occasion it was decorated with flowers by negro girls, and that former gay and refined audience was replaced by a motley throng of negroes, and the poor old stage where Capt. Gary, young and enthusiastic—poor fellow, he long ago filled a bloody grave—banner in hand spouted fire and fury about patriotism and swore so many things about their flag—think in contrast of those orators of yesterday!

After all the speeches were ended, I hear Col. Haughton gave them some very welcome advice. They repaired to their dinner which was spread in the woods just out of town. The dinner was on a grand scale, and after it was over the guests began dancing. They had asked Col. Haughton's permission to follow the example of the Charleston negroes and bury slavery with pomp and ceremony, but the Colonel refused, advising them to wait till they were absolutely certain that they were free permanently before burying slavery.

Thanks to Col. Haughton, everything was quiet and orderly. But for the crowds and dust one would not have imagined the Fourth was being celebrated. After nightfall they returned and from the common opposite the Campus sent off fireworks while a brass band played continuously. I watched the fireworks from the front door for a little while, but I could not stand it. It was too humiliating and made me realize our condition too keenly. When the pyrotechnics were exhausted, the band ceased and the negroes were left to make their own music. Hundreds of voices singing strange negro songs and hundreds of feet dancing weird negro dances made a terrible noise. They were still dancing when Col. Haughton returned about twelve o'clock and put an end to their frolic, when we were able to sleep.

We are very fortunate in having Col. Haughton here. As far as lay in his power, he has tried to reduce the anarchy and confusion to something like order. He has been all kindness and consideration to the citizens. The negroes dislike him, and say he is no Yankee but half a rebel. It goes against the grain to admit anything good of a Yankee, but I have to own that he has acted well towards us. He is a Western man, which may partly account for it. Like all Westerners, he is rough, unpolished and not highly educated, but he seems to have the instincts of a gentleman, and although he evidently feels the coldness with which he is treated, he yet seems to have some slight idea of what our feelings must be and does not vent his spite for not being received socially. Hartwell and Hatch leave today, but the former leaves orders with Haughton to hold Mrs. Bausket's house and not allow her to remove anything from it. She is not even allowed to enter it. Kate B. has a permit from Col. Haughton to enter her *father's* house and remove her *personal* effects. What tyranny! Col. H. is distressed about it and perhaps his intercessions may finally avail to have the house restored to her.

AUGUST 6TH. SUNDAY. It has been a month since I have made an entry in this journal. But our home life is monotonous with little worth recording. And as to the condition of the country and our unhappy state as a people, it would seem better not to think of that, still less to write of it. It makes me miserable and intensifies the wicked feelings I have too much anyway. I try as hard as I can to fill my mind with other things to the exclusion of such. As far as I can, I try to lose myself in books and study.

Aunt Jane and Cousin Ada left last Saturday (yesterday). They had received their transportation, but had not expected to leave for a week or two. While at the dinner table, however, they suddenly received notice from Col. Haughton that the wagons would leave early next morning. At eight o'clock their conveyance was at the door in the shape of a rough covered wagon. In this, after hurried adieus from all of us, they were soon seated. 'Pretty rough travelling for ladies,' said the Yankee who stood near assisting them. And indeed it was, but they had a taste of the same kind of travelling in their hegira from Liberty County. They hope to reach Orangeburg this afternoon where they take the cars to Charleston, thence by steamer to Savannah, arriving there probably on Wednesday—from Savannah by wagon out to the plantation (about thirty miles).

We think it rather dangerous to venture on the plantation at this season, especially as Aunt Jane is still hardly strong—it seems most unwise. We expected her to remain in Columbia until November, spending the next three months with us, but as soon as she heard that Cousin Annie had persisted in her resolution to accompany her husband, Dr. Adams, down there, she declared she must be with her daughter and off she started.

It seems a great piece of folly for Cousin Annie in her present condition to go to that debilitating climate and risk malaria, but, of course, it is natural that her mother should feel she must be with her. They will at least be eaten up by mosquitoes. Speaking of this pest, we have scarcely felt one this summer—I wonder if it is because there are no railroads to bring them up from the coast. Another notable event since my last entry is Miss Mary's departure for the North. Her annuity has accumulated during the war and she went on about three weeks ago to see about getting it. She sent back a large part of it to Aunt Josie's family in the shape of clothing.

It was a sight indeed to our eyes to behold new dresses! Just to touch an organdie, and silks! The freshness of them! How really beautiful they looked. How many years it seemed since we even dreamed of a new frock finer than homespun or at most calico! She had promised Sallie and me a new dress apiece, but luckily I had built no hopes upon her promises for I knew she would need all she had to supply Aunt Josie, so I was not disappointed, but poor Sallie was bitterly so. She had dreamed of a white dress to wear to her little dances. She sent me a white tulle bonnet trimmed with pale lilac (!) which not only goes ill with my complexion, but is most strangely out of harmony with my other clothes. It will be laid aside for future consideration. Aunt Jane and Cousin Ada got a new muslin apiece, and Father a felt hat—I was surely glad of that, for certainly his old one was most disgraceful. A new hat, though, looks rather odd with his old clothes. Oh, that abominable old suit! It hangs lankly on him, innocent of any fit, and of such dingy hue. His skin is tanned by exposure last winter, and hair, face and garments all seem nearly the same color. It is well a gentleman nowadays is not judged by his exterior.

As for me, I can get on very well through the summer if only I had a white muslin to wait on Mary Palmer in—she is to be married next month and has asked me to be her bridesmaid. As to how I have passed my time during the past month, there is little to tell. One day is like another, but for the French one day and German the next. Kate B. asked me to read with her and I do it to oblige her, feeling it a great waste of time to be going over one of Scott's novels that I have already read. But on the other hand I am too selfish anyway. Yet with studying the time that is left seems rather precious and that is why I really have dropped this diary.

'What Tyranny'

AUGUST IOTH. Our provisional Governor Perry[9] is here—Gilmore and eight other generals are here to meet him, to have a grand consultation. The town, or at least the Campus, is swarming with those detestable blue coats, and negro soldiers pass and repass.

Perry has been empowered by Johnson to act as he pleases with the exception of remanding the negroes to slavery. Their fine President seems disposed to adopt a conciliatory policy. Perhaps he feels a spark of attachment for the State where he once plied his trade as tailor. I believe he used to make Gov. Perry's clothes for him. I am pleased to say, however, that South Carolina has not the honor of having given birth to this appropriate Yankee President. He is a North Carolinian.

The Convention meets in September. What a contrast it will present to the one that assembled in 1860! [10]

9. Benjamin F. Perry

10. In 1866 the College reopened. Carpetbaggers insisted that Negroes be admitted, and white students and white faculty soon left in a body. Because of Joseph LeConte's activities in behalf of the Confederacy, no academic door seemed open to him. But at this time the University of California was being founded, and here there was no deep prejudice. Harvard's celebrated Louis Agassiz led the group that endorsed Joseph LeConte as one of the country's fine scientists, and in 1869 he traveled the Overland Trail to California to occupy the chair of geology at the new university. Many years of productive research followed—Joseph LeConte was especially renowned for his studies of mountain structure and earthquakes—and the difference between this new life and the old would be revealed that first Christmas in California when Carrie saw "a huge box of toys. 'Why, Papa, I never heard of Santa Claus before! Why didn't Santa Claus come to the little boys and girls in Columbia?' I looked up and wondered why my father's and mother's eyes were filled with tears."

End of the diary.

ADDED NOTE: The marriage of Mary Palmer took place in the early Fall. I did somehow manage to get the white muslin for the occasion—my first party! Aunt Josie dressed my hair and put in a pretty spray of artificial white roses. I have a vivid memory of the unfortunate young man who was the groomsman with me, but have forgotten his name. He was probably a young Presbyterian theolog—and as ill at ease as was I.

INDEX

Index

Index

Index